LEADING THE WAY THROUGH

GALATIANS

LEADING THE WAY THROUGH

GALATIANS

MICHAEL YOUSSEF

HARVEST HOUSE PUBLISHERS
EUGENE, OREGON

Cover design by Harvest House Publishers, Inc., Eugene, Oregon

Cover photos © iStockphoto/ kBarcin, BrianAJackson

Published in association with the literary agency of Wolgemuth & Associates., Inc.

Leading the Way Through Galatians
Copyright © 2013 by Michael Youssef
Published by Harvest House Publishers
Eugene, Oregon 97402
www.harvesthousepublishers.com

Library of Congress Cataloging-in-Publication Data

Youssef, Michael.
 Leading the way through Galatians / Michael Youssef.
  p. cm.
ISBN 978-0-7369-5166-1 (pbk.)
ISBN 978-0-7369-5167-8 (eBook)
1. Bible. N.T. Galatians—Commentaries. I. Title.
BS2685.53.Y68 2013
227'.407—dc23
                    2012031473

To all faithful preachers, teachers, and Christian leaders
who seek to accurately expound the Word of God
from pulpits or in Sunday school classes or in home Bible study groups.

Acknowledgments

I want to offer all my thanksgiving to the Father in heaven whose Holy Spirit has laid on my heart the writing of this series for the glory of Jesus. I am also immensely grateful to the Lord for sending me an able and gifted editor and compiler of my material in Jim Denney.

Special thanks to the entire team at Harvest House—and especially to Bob Hawkins Jr., LaRae Weikert, and Rod Morris, who shared my vision and made this dream a reality.

My expression of thanks would not be complete without mentioning the patience and perseverance of Robert and Andrew Wolgemuth of Wolgemuth & Associates, Inc., for managing the many details of such an undertaking.

My earnest prayer is that, as I leave this legacy to the next generation, God would raise up great men and women to faithfully serve their generation by accurately interpreting the Word of God.

Contents

Introduction

Paul's Declaration of Liberation

Galatians has been called "the Magna Carta of Spiritual Liberty," "the Battle Cry of the Reformation," and "Paul's Fighting Epistle." I like to think of Galatians as "Paul's Declaration of Liberation."

The message of Galatians is the good news of our spiritual freedom in Christ. It has been nearly two thousand years since the apostle Paul, under the inspiration of the Holy Spirit, set forth this amazing declaration of Christian liberty. Yet the message of Galatians is as relevant today as when the ink was still wet on the parchment.

People today worship at the altar of so-called freedom, yet they are ignorant of what it means to be truly free in Christ. They demand their personal liberty, yet they reject knowledge of the true Liberator. The more they indulge their "freedom," the more enslaved they become to sin and addiction. In Galatians, you'll learn what it means to be truly liberated, and you'll learn how to communicate this message of freedom to those around you who are slaves to the law, slaves to the flesh, slaves to their own self-destructive impulses and desires.

Paul's letter to the Christians in Galatia is very different from most of his other letters. Whereas most of his letters were addressed to either individuals (Timothy, Titus, Philemon) or churches in specific cities (Romans, Ephesians, Philippians), Galatians is addressed to a number of churches across a wide region. Ancient Galatia was a region in the Anatolian highlands of present-day Turkey. In Acts 13 and 14, we find that the Galatian churches were planted in the region by Paul and Barnabas on Paul's first missionary journey.

Paul and Barnabas encountered severe resistance during their travels through Galatia. They were persecuted in the Galatian cities of Antioch, Iconium, and Derbe. In Lystra, Paul and Barnabas were initially welcomed as gods: "Barnabas they called Zeus, and Paul, Hermes, because he was the chief speaker" (Acts 14:12). Later, persecutors arrived from other cities and stirred up the crowds against Paul. The crowds stoned Paul and dragged him outside the city. Though Paul seemed dead, he later rose up and went on to Derbe with Barnabas. Despite intense resistance to the gospel, Paul, led by the Holy Spirit, planted a number of churches in that region.

On Paul's second missionary journey, accompanied by Silas, he visited the churches he and Barnabas had established in the region. During that second journey, he spent considerable time recuperating from an illness. Paul refers to this illness here in his letter to the Galatians, and his wording suggests that his illness probably had to do with his eyes:

> You know it was because of a bodily ailment that I preached the gospel to you at first, and though my condition was a trial to you, you did not scorn or despise me, but received me as an angel of God, as Christ Jesus. What then has become of your blessedness? For I testify to you

that, if possible, you would have gouged out your eyes and
given them to me (4:13-15).

Paul's feelings for the churches in Galatia were intensified by
the strong emotions of his experiences in that region. In Galatia,
he was persecuted, stoned, and nearly killed, yet he was also loved
and cared for by the believers in these young churches. He suffered
from a bodily ailment that, in some way, was a trial for the Galatian
Christians to endure—perhaps because Paul's ailment made him
unpleasant to look at. In spite of his affliction, the Galatian Christians treated him as if he were an angel from God.

In Galatians, Paul expresses some of the most practical and powerful themes of the Christian life:

- The revealed gospel of grace is far different from the false
  gospel of legalism.
- Substituting works in place of grace nullifies the Lord's
  sacrifice on the cross.
- Even Abraham was saved by grace through faith, not by
  works or the law.
- False teachers serve themselves, not God.
- The law is not an end in itself, but a guardian or tutor to
  drive us to grace.
- We are to live as children of the promise, not as children
  of the flesh.
- We are to live by the fruit of the Spirit and not by the
  works of the flesh.
- Be kind and concerned for one another, sharing each
  other's burdens.

Now, turn the page with me, and together let's plunge into the
depths of this great reservoir of God's truth for our lives, Paul's letter to the Galatians.

1

Liberated in Christ— or Slaves to Ritual?

Galatians 1:1-9

Mohandas K. Gandhi led the Indian nationalist movement in British-ruled India in the early twentieth century. His example inspired nonviolent freedom movements across the world, including the civil rights movement in the United States. Gandhi was a Hindu, but he was also an admirer of the words and life of Jesus Christ. There's a saying often attributed to Gandhi, and though I cannot confirm that he actually said it, it is certainly consistent with other statements he has made: "I like your Christ, but I do not like your Christians. Your Christians are so unlike your Christ."

If only Christians would be more like Christ!

Even one of the world's most scathing atheists has expressed a reluctant admiration for the Lord Jesus. Though biologist Richard Dawkins regularly accuses Christians of hypocrisy, in *The God Delusion* he writes: "Jesus, if he existed…was surely one of the great ethical innovators of history. The Sermon on the Mount is way ahead of its time. His 'turn the other cheek' anticipated Gandhi and Martin Luther King by two thousand years."[1]

As Christians, let's not be defensive and let's not be hypocritical. When people outside the church call Christians "hypocrites," their criticism is all too often true. None of us can claim to always live up to the teachings of Jesus—and many of us have to admit that we regularly fall far short of the Lord's teachings.

Look at our hypocrisy as Christians: We are offended by profanity and obscenity (as we should be), yet we wink at the sin of pride (especially our own). We condemn lust and sex outside of marriage (as well we should), but we eagerly engage in gossip, slander, and backbiting and justify it as "telephone ministry." We condemn the sins of passion, yet we rationalize the sins of a bitter disposition. We speak the language of heaven on Sunday, and breathe hellfire the rest of the week. We speak of the sweetness of knowing Christ, yet we walk around looking as if we've been baptized in vinegar.

A friend of mine, a former pastor of a prominent church, told me that he once moved the doxology from one part of the worship service to another. He didn't leave out the doxology and he didn't change the wording of the doxology—he simply moved it to a different place in the order of worship. He received twenty-four letters of complaint!

We claim we are saved by grace through faith in Jesus alone, yet if the pastor makes the slightest change in our churchly rituals, we treat it as the vilest form of heresy. And we wonder why the world tells us that the church is no longer relevant—and why the two fastest-growing worldviews in America today are Islam and atheism.

The world views Christianity as a culture, if not a cult, of hypocrisy and legalism. We are more interested in enforcing certain legalistic rules than in enjoying the liberating presence of the Holy Spirit.

As Paul told the believers in Corinth, "Now the Lord is the Spirit, and where the Spirit of the Lord is, there is freedom" (2 Corinthians 3:17).

Instead of the Spirit of the Lord, the spirit of hypocrisy and legalism reigns supreme across much of our evangelical culture today—and this spirit is hindering the work of the Holy Spirit. God doesn't want to see his people bound up in legalistic rules and rituals.

Jesus warned against the hypocrisy and legalism of the scribes and Pharisees when he told the crowd:

> "The scribes and the Pharisees sit on Moses' seat, so do and observe whatever they tell you, but not the works they do. For they preach, but do not practice. They tie up heavy burdens, hard to bear, and lay them on people's shoulders, but they themselves are not willing to move them with their finger...
>
> But woe to you, scribes and Pharisees, hypocrites! For you shut the kingdom of heaven in people's faces. For you neither enter yourselves nor allow those who would enter to go in" (Matthew 23:2-4,13).

Like the Lord Jesus, the apostle Paul warns against religious hypocrisy and legalism. As we will see in Galatians 2, trying to save ourselves through legalistic rituals has the opposite effect: it nullifies the grace of God, because "if righteousness were through the law, then Christ died for no purpose" (2:21). In other words, if we were able to save ourselves through our own observance of rules and rituals, then Jesus died in vain.

I can't imagine any more horrible thought than that Jesus might have died for nothing. What a terrible sin we would commit if we canceled out God's grace and rendered the death of Jesus on the cross meaningless—completely null and void. And yet that's exactly the sin many people in the church commit to this day.

Jesus battled legalism throughout his earthly ministry. He stood up to the hatred, hypocrisy, and legalism of the scribes and Pharisees, and that is why they plotted to kill him. Legalism gave them power over the people, and Jesus threatened that power.

Legalism is the theology of Satan. When we practice hypocritical legalism in the evangelical community, we literally put Satan in charge of the church.

The apostle of grace versus false teachers of the law

Paul opens the letter by stating his credentials as an apostle. The word *apostle* literally means "ambassador" or "messenger," one who was sent to another place as a personal representative. Paul, the apostle, was God's ambassador who personally represented God to the churches. That is Paul's authority. Paul writes:

> Paul, an apostle—not from men nor through man, but through Jesus Christ and God the Father, who raised him from the dead—and all the brothers who are with me,
> To the churches of Galatia:
> Grace to you and peace from God our Father and the Lord Jesus Christ, who gave himself for our sins to deliver us from the present evil age, according to the will of our God and Father, to whom be the glory forever and ever. Amen (1:1-5).

Whenever the apostle Paul wrote letters to the churches, such as in Rome or Ephesus or Philippi, he began by thanking God for the people in that church. He even expressed thankfulness for the church in Corinth, a church that would have made headlines for its scandalous behavior. But when Paul wrote to the churches in Galatia, he didn't express gratitude. His greeting—the first five verses of Galatians—starts out cordially enough. But beginning at verse 6, Paul lowers the boom:

> I am astonished that you are so quickly deserting him
> who called you in the grace of Christ and are turning to a
> different gospel—not that there is another one, but there
> are some who trouble you and want to distort the gospel
> of Christ. But even if we or an angel from heaven should
> preach to you a gospel contrary to the one we preached
> to you, let him be accursed. As we have said before, so
> now I say again: If anyone is preaching to you a gospel con-
> trary to the one you received, let him be accursed (1:6-9).

The tone Paul takes in these verses makes this letter completely unlike all of his other letters. Here he is emotional, intense, at times angry—indeed, almost violently so! Later in this letter, we will see Paul expressing his wrath toward a group of people called Judaizers. These people had an outward profession of Christianity, yet they insisted on imposing the old rituals and rules of Judaism on the church. The Judaizers taught a perverted and false version of Paul's gospel. They belittled Paul's teachings, claiming that a gospel of salvation by grace alone was not sufficient to save.

The Christians in the Galatian churches were almost entirely Gentiles, people who had never been steeped in the traditions of the Jewish faith. Paul had converted them out of paganism, and now they embraced the liberating grace of faith in Jesus Christ. But suddenly these legalistic Judaizers had come to them preaching that they were not complete as Christians until they adopted all the old rules and rituals of Judaism. According to the Judaizers, these Gentile Christians in Galatia needed to be circumcised, keep the law of Moses, and obey all the rituals and rules of the Old Testament.

What about Jesus? What about his death on the cross? The Judaizers said, yes, it's important to have faith in Jesus—but you are not truly complete as a Christian unless you obey the Old Testament law. That's why Paul says in these verses that these Judaizers "want to distort the gospel of Christ." These hypocritical Judaizers were telling the new converts that:

- Jesus alone is not enough.
- Repentance and forgiveness are not enough.
- The gospel is incomplete and inadequate without the ceremonial laws.

The Judaizers also practiced a dishonest form of argument called *ad hominem* attack (from the Latin for "against the man"). They sought to undermine the gospel message by attacking the messenger, the apostle Paul. If they could undermine his authority, then they could cast doubt on the validity of the gospel of grace. So these Judaizers were telling the Galatian believers that Paul was not a true apostle because he wasn't one of the original Twelve. They claimed that he had appointed himself without having any legitimate credentials.

People today still use personal attacks in an attempt to undermine the teaching of the apostle Paul. I've heard feminists in the church today refer to Paul as a "woman hater." They vilify Paul in order to plant the notion in unsuspecting minds that Paul's teaching (rooted in Genesis 3) lacks authority as Scripture. Their goal is to make it easier to dismiss the biblical teaching of a husband's spiritual headship in the home. In this way, they can elevate the authority of secular feminist values over the authority of Paul's teaching in Scripture.

When people don't have facts, authority, and logic on their side, they invariably resort to personal attacks. The Judaizers were no exception. They condemned Paul for not being one of the original Twelve, claiming he was therefore not qualified as an apostle and his teaching was not valid. But what qualified the Judaizers to condemn Paul? What validation did they offer for their so-called gospel? Had they walked with Jesus? Were they apostles? Of course not.

Isn't it amazing that people often accuse others of not having what they themselves lack? These self-appointed, nonapostolic, uncommissioned "teachers" accused Paul of being self-appointed, nonapostolic, and uncommissioned! Yet Paul had actually been commissioned and appointed as an apostle in the most dramatic way imaginable: Jesus himself, the risen Lord, confronted Paul face-to-face on the road to Damascus (see Acts 9:1-9).

So Paul, in the very first verse of this letter, sets forth his credentials as an apostle: "Paul, an apostle—not from men nor through man, but through Jesus Christ and God the Father, who raised him from the dead." Or, to paraphrase that verse, "The Lord Jesus and God the Father appointed me as an apostle of the gospel, so you can tell all those weasels who are spreading lies about me to put a sock in it!"

Paul wants the Galatian Christians to know that the gospel he preached to them from the beginning is the full, complete, and one-and-only gospel of Jesus Christ. As for the false and legalistic gospel of the Judaizers, Paul does not mince words: "But even if we or an angel from heaven should preach to you a gospel contrary to the one we preached to you, let him be accursed. As we have said before, so now I say again: If anyone is preaching to you a gospel contrary to the one you received, let him be accursed."

These are blunt words. The apostle does not want anyone to mistake his meaning. The word *accursed* refers to eternal damnation. To paraphrase Paul, he is saying that anyone who preaches a distorted gospel, a gospel that is different from the one Paul originally preached, should be condemned to hell. Paul goes so far as to say that even if he himself now preached a different gospel from the gospel of grace he had originally preached, he too should be condemned! Paul leaves no doubt as to how strongly he feels about those who would corrupt the gospel of salvation through faith in Jesus Christ.

Some of us might wince at Paul's bluntness, at the intensity of this curse. But Paul is not being rude or profane. He is speaking as God's ambassador, inspired by the Spirit of God. It was God himself who sent Jesus to bring grace, forgiveness, and salvation to the human race, and Paul speaks for God when he says that those who would corrupt the good news of Jesus Christ deserve absolute condemnation.

So there is a fiery intensity that burns hotly throughout Paul's letter to the Galatian churches. Paul is deeply disturbed by the hypocrisy, legalism, deception, and false teachings that had infected these churches he had planted. Paul reflects the intensity of God, who does not want to see the good news of Jesus Christ perverted, and who does not want to see these young churches enslaved by hypocritical legalism.

The Judaizers in the Galatian churches are no different from the scribes and Pharisees that Jesus confronted when he said, "But woe to you, scribes and Pharisees, hypocrites! For you shut the kingdom of heaven in people's faces. For you neither enter yourselves nor allow those who would enter to go in." The destructive spirit of hypocritical legalism was pervasive in Jesus's day and in Paul's day, and it is active in our day as well.

The sweet, pure message of the gospel is so simple that Paul summed it up in a single phrase in verses 3 and 4: "Grace to you and peace from God our Father and the Lord Jesus Christ, who gave himself for our sins to deliver us from the present evil age." Jesus gave himself for our sins—he justified and saved us. And Jesus is delivering us from this present evil age—that's sanctification, a gradual process of being made holy and Christlike in our character. This simple gospel is entirely a matter of God's grace, not of any works of our own.

Again and again throughout Galatians, we're going to see the intensity of Paul's passion for defending the purity of the gospel of

Jesus Christ. For example, when we come to Galatians 3:1, we'll hear Paul shout, "O foolish Galatians! Who has bewitched you?" Why was Paul so intense and angry with these churches? There was no suggestion of adultery, drunkenness, and embezzling in Galatia as there was in the church at Corinth—yet Paul expressed more outrage toward the Galatians than he did toward the extravagant scandals of the Corinthians.

What was the sin of the Galatian churches? What made Paul so angry?

Legalism! The Galatians had become so wrapped up in dead rituals and useless traditions that legalism had become their "gospel." The Galatians had nullified the grace of God—and if the grace of God has been nullified, then Christ has died in vain. Paul wrote the letter of Galatians to correct this spiritually dangerous situation.

A message of grace and peace

After asserting his authority as a true apostle, sent by the risen Christ to preach the gospel, Paul goes on to establish the two pillars on which the gospel stands. Those two pillars are grace and peace:

> Grace to you and peace from God our Father and the Lord Jesus Christ, who gave himself for our sins to deliver us from the present evil age, according to the will of our God and Father, to whom be the glory forever and ever. Amen (1:3-5).

Grace and peace! These are two of the most precious words in the Christian life. Grace is the source of our salvation. Peace is the result of our salvation. Grace and peace flow together from God our Father through his Son, the Lord Jesus Christ.

The heart of the gospel is that Jesus Christ willingly sacrificed himself for our sins. His sacrifice is not only *sufficient* to save us from our sins, but is the *only* thing that can save us from our sins. You cannot be saved by willpower or by the effort to resist sinful habits and eradicate sin from your life. You cannot be saved by doing good works, giving to charity, or observing religious rituals. You cannot be saved by becoming better educated, reforming your ways, reading self-help books, or attending self-improvement seminars. Salvation is through Jesus Christ alone. As Paul wrote to the Ephesians, "For by grace you have been saved through faith. And this is not your own doing; it is the gift of God, not a result of works, so that no one may boast" (Ephesians 2:8-9).

Jesus did all the work for our salvation. That is God's grace to us. Our response is simply to trust in God's promise to forgive our sins according to the work of Jesus Christ on the cross.

Many people would like to separate Christ from the cross. They would like to focus on the teachings, the love, the kindness, and the compassion of Jesus while setting aside the cross and the resurrection. They claim that it's enough to simply try to follow the teachings of Jesus without believing that he is the Word made flesh, that his death atones for our sins, and that his resurrection brings us eternal life.

But take away the cross and the resurrection, and the earthly ministry of Jesus Christ—his teachings, his acts of compassion, and his miracles—would all be meaningless. Without the cross and the resurrection, Jesus would have no more power to save than Buddha, Krishna, or Muhammad—"prophets" who founded religions, but who had no power to save even themselves.

The salvation Jesus purchased for us on the cross is, Paul tells us, a heroic act of rescue. Jesus rescued us from this present evil age and delivered us to eternal life. He rescued us from eternal judgment in hell and delivered us to eternal bliss in heaven. He rescued us from the punishment we deserve and delivered us to a reward of unmerited grace.

It has become increasingly unpopular to talk about hell in evangelical Christian circles today. A recent book by a popular author promotes the idea that the Bible doesn't really mean what it says about hell. He claims that biblical references to hell can be interpreted in a variety of ways, including a notion (known as "universal reconciliation") that the author describes this way: "Hell is not forever, and love, in the end, wins and all will be reconciled to God."

The author would like us to believe that his views are actually in the mainstream of orthodox Christian tradition. In the introduction to his book, he writes, "I haven't come up with a radical new teaching that's any kind of departure from what's been said an untold number of times. That's the beauty of the historic, orthodox Christian faith. It's a deep, wide, diverse stream that's been flowing for thousands of years, carrying a staggering variety of voices, perspectives, and experiences."

This man's teaching may not be new (it is, in fact, an ancient heresy), but it is clearly not historic, orthodox Christianity. For these past twenty centuries, orthodox Christianity has rejected this notion as apostasy. If we claim to follow the teachings of Jesus, then we have no choice but to reject the teachings of those who bring a different gospel, a "gospel" of so-called "universal reconciliation." If hell is not forever and all will be reconciled to God, then why did Jesus say, "Do not fear those who kill the body but cannot kill the soul. Rather fear him who can destroy both soul and body in hell" (Matthew 10:28)? As you read through the Gospels, you cannot help being struck by the fact that Jesus has more to say about eternal judgment in hell than all the rest of the New Testament writers put together.

Is the doctrine of hell troubling and disturbing to the soul? Absolutely! For in the final analysis, the question is why would God, who is all-loving and all-powerful, not forcefully stop people from choosing to suffer an eternity in hell? But my thoughts and questions are unimportant. The Word of God is the Word of God regardless of what anyone else thinks or feels.

I choose to trust in the wisdom, justice, and love of God. Instead of embracing unbiblical universalism, I choose to follow the example of Jesus himself. I choose to call people to faith in Christ, preaching the promise of eternal rewards while warning of the terrors of eternal judgment. Jesus is the only one who can rescue us from hell and from this present evil age.

Jesus plus nothing

The natural direction of the world is toward eternal judgment. Those who have lived their lives according to the false values of this present age are on a constantly moving conveyor belt that leads to hell—a place Jesus described (citing Isaiah 66:24) as "where 'the worms that eat them do not die, and the fire is not quenched'" (Mark 9:48 NIV).

That's why the apostle Paul is absolutely flabbergasted and astonished at the Galatians' turnaround. They had already boarded the rescue ship that would take them away from hell and damnation and would lead them to the safe harbor of heaven. Yet many had leaped overboard, following the false teachers who claimed that Jesus and the cross were not sufficient for salvation.

Here is an important principle for all believers to heed: Satan and his emissaries seek to deceive us through other human beings—and most especially through so-called "religious leaders." Paul, in Galatians 2:4, calls them "false brothers secretly brought in—who slipped in to spy out our freedom that we have in Christ Jesus, so that they might bring us into slavery."

How can you tell the difference between a true teacher and a false teacher? Paul gives us a simple litmus test:

> [Y]et we know that a person is not justified by works of the law but through faith in Jesus Christ, so we also have believed in Christ Jesus, in order to be justified by faith in Christ and not by works of the law, because by works of the law no one will be justified (2:16).

In other words, we know that we are saved by faith in Jesus alone. If anyone tells you that you can be saved through Jesus *plus* keeping the ceremonial law, that person is a false teacher. If anyone tells you that you can be saved through Jesus *plus* baptism or receiving communion, that person is a false teacher. If anyone tells you that you can be saved through Jesus *plus* a certain style of worship or observing certain rituals, that person is a false teacher. If anyone tells you that you can be saved through Jesus *plus* belonging to a certain "one true church," that person is a false teacher. If anyone tells you that salvation is a matter of Jesus *plus* anything else, that person is a false teacher.

A righteous and godly way of life is an important evidence that we belong to God, but our righteous actions cannot save us. Baptism and holy communion are important symbols of our faith and reminders of our identification with Christ's death and resurrection, but these symbols cannot save us. Certain rituals and forms of worship can help us to focus our minds and hearts on God, but rituals cannot save us.

Salvation is a matter of *Jesus plus nothing*. Anyone who preaches a gospel different from that is a false teacher.

There is a saying among some liberal theologians and clergy: "Doctrine divides; sacraments unite." In other words, it doesn't matter what you believe; all that matters is that you go through the motions of the sacraments. Ritual trumps spiritual reality. I'm convinced that Satan achieves his most effective work through the deceptive teachings of false teachers who pretend to speak for God.

Look at the history of Israel. Whenever the priests and kings of Israel compromised God's truth, the people of Israel fell into idolatry and pagan practices.

We see this principle throughout the book of Judges, which is a record of repeated compromise and moral failure, resulting in the steady decline of the nation of Israel. The nation repeatedly disobeyed God, intermarrying with the Canaanites, sacrificing to their demon gods, and compromising with the godless world around them.

Solomon, the wisest man who ever lived, became a fool at the end of his life. He compromised with the world by marrying pagan wives—and they seduced him into compromising his faith and sacrificing to false gods. As a result of Solomon's compromise, the splendor of Israel faded, the kingdom was divided, and most of the kings who descended from Solomon were evil men who led the nation into spiritual, moral, and economic decline.

One of Israel's evil kings, Ahaz (2 Kings 16), actually sacrificed his own son to the demon-god Moloch and desecrated the temple of Solomon. After a long succession of mostly wicked kings, God finally permitted the Assyrians to conquer the northern kingdom (Israel) and permitted the Babylonians to conquer the southern kingdom (Judah).

When Israel was unfaithful to God, the change never came about abruptly. The unfaithfulness of Israel always began with small steps of compromise. The Israelites never said, "Let's abandon God and begin serving Moloch." Instead, they would say, "We serve the Lord God—but it doesn't hurt to worship Moloch now and then too. It's okay to have an altar to the Canaanite gods on one of the high places. We believe in tolerance toward other cultures, ideas, and religions. We believe in reasonable compromise."

But compromise leads to apostasy. You cannot serve both God and idols. You must choose. God still sets the same choice before us today. He will not let us live a life of compromise. We cannot serve both God and money. We cannot serve both God and worldly ambition. We cannot serve both God and pride. We cannot serve both God and selfish glory. We cannot serve both God and friendship with the world.

We cannot compromise; we must choose.

A church in decline

We need to wake up and look around and realize that what happened in Israel in the Old Testament is now happening to churches in the twenty-first century. America was once a godly nation, founded on Christian principles. I'm not saying that the founding fathers were all evangelical Christians, but they all respected the role of Judeo-Christian principles and the Christian faith in the life of the nation.

George Washington in his farewell address (September 19, 1796), said, "Of all the dispositions and habits which lead to political prosperity, religion and morality are indispensable supports. In vain would that man claim the tribute of Patriotism, who should labor to subvert these great pillars of human happiness, these firmest props of the duties of Man and citizens."[2]

And John Adams, addressing the Massachusetts militia in 1798, said, "Our constitution was made only for a moral and religious people. It is wholly inadequate for the government of any other."

The first chief justice of the Supreme Court, John Jay, wrote in 1797, "Providence has given to our people the choice of their rulers, and it is the duty, as well as the privilege and interest of our Christian nation to select and prefer Christians for their rulers."[3]

But the godly practices and Christian principles that our nation was founded on have steadily eroded. America is now in decline. Our government and our economy teeter on the brink of collapse due to trillions of dollars of unsustainable debt. Our economic growth is anemic, and we have lost our global competitiveness. Our education system is in decay; we graduate children who cannot read their own diplomas. American fifteen-year-olds score in the bottom half of all advanced nations in math and science literacy.[4] The American people have become slaves to their own debt; they owe far more on their homes than the properties can be sold for.

The nation that put men on the moon can now no longer afford a manned space program. As one commentator noted, "The manned space program was a great accomplishment, and it's now in decline and disintegrating."[5] America could never launch a program as ambitious as the Apollo mission or the space shuttle program in today's economic climate—and that is because America is in decline.

I attribute America's decline to the corrosive effect of spiritual and moral compromise. Greed has replaced charity. License has replaced liberty. Pride has replaced prudence. We now tolerate every form of excess, obscenity, vulgarity, immorality, and godlessness. In fact, we are tolerant of practically anything except the Christian faith and its moral principles—the voice of faith must be throttled and silenced! We teach our children that the solution to unwanted pregnancies is not abstinence but abortion. The welfare state we have created is killing human initiative, encouraging generational dependency, destroying families, and trapping children in a life of poverty.

What happened to America? Why is our culture in moral free fall?

Let's not point fingers of blame at the godless people in our society. As John R.W. Stott once observed, "We should not ask, 'What is wrong with the world?' for that diagnosis has already been given. Rather we should ask, 'What has happened to salt and light?'"[6] Godless people are just doing what godless people naturally do. The problem is not the world. The problem is the church. We in the church, including many leaders and teachers and preachers, have compromised God's truth. We have tolerated sin. We have questioned the authenticity of God's Word, and we have undermined its authority.

Just as the Judaizers in the Galatian churches taught that salvation is a matter of Christ *plus* works, many in the church today have debated and questioned the doctrine of the sufficiency of Christ. Many teach that our message is not a gospel of salvation by grace through faith in Jesus Christ; they say instead that the church should preach a social gospel consisting largely of the "progressive" political agenda—enlarging the welfare state, amnesty for illegal immigrants, socialized medicine, green environmental policy, and so forth.

Many so-called Christian leaders today seek the favor of men above the favor of God and the purity of God's truth. In order to maintain their popularity and approval in a godless world, they have watered down the truth of God's Word. In our evangelical seminaries, we have allowed radical professors to attack and "deconstruct" God's Word from a variety of worldly perspectives, including postmodernism, feminism, liberation theology, and even atheism and agnosticism.

All of these babbling voices seem bent on one goal: undermining the biblical doctrine of salvation by grace through faith in Jesus Christ. I would go so far as to say that Satan himself is behind this effort to confuse the church about the central issue of our faith. Satan knows that if he can sow confusion in the minds of Christians over what salvation is and how salvation is attained, then he can neutralize the effectiveness and influence of the church.

People sometimes come to me and say, "I'm not sure if my minister is preaching God's truth or not. Is there some way I can tell if my minister believes and preaches the pure Word of God?"

I reply, "There is a simple test. Ask your minister this question: 'Is Jesus Christ the one and only way to heaven?' If he answers yes, then he is preaching God's truth. If he answers no, he is not preaching God's truth. He is preaching a different gospel. If he waffles, if he hems and haws, or if he gives you a long, complicated answer that is difficult to understand, then keep asking for a yes or no answer."

Grace is the essence of the gospel. The gospel message is that Jesus Christ is the way to salvation—Jesus *plus* nothing else.

Don't be misled!

Galatians is the most intense and fiery epistle in the New Testament. Paul is filled with righteous indignation! His words are like a sword that cuts cleanly, dividing right from wrong, truth from error, gospel from lie. He wants the believers in Galatia to know that religious ritualism and legalism are powerless to save. Religious works cannot move us from death to life, cannot give us power over sin, cannot remove the punishment of sin, and cannot deliver us from the present evil age and take us to heaven.

Paul was angry—righteously, rightfully angry—that false teachers had invaded the churches he had planted. These false Christians had brought confusion into the minds and hearts of people he himself had led to the Lord.

Many people today are in the same predicament as the Galatian Christians. They have received the pure gospel of Jesus Christ.

They have placed their trust and faith in him. Then they hear a false teacher speak or read a book by a false teacher or attend a class led by a false teacher who says that salvation is Jesus *plus* something else or that God is too big to allow only one way to heaven.

Don't be misled; don't be confused. The Christian gospel consists of Jesus and *only* Jesus and *nothing but* Jesus.

The greatest danger you face as a Christian is not atheism or agnosticism or paganism or Wicca or Satanism or Eastern mysticism. The greatest danger you face as a Christian comes from "Christians" who subtly deny the authority of Scripture. They won't attack your faith bluntly and boldly. They will gently try to undermine your faith, poke holes in your faith, or add something to your faith as the Judaizers did. They will convince you that having a positive outlook on life is the source of your salvation.

One small amount of yeast can leaven all the dough. One bad apple can spread its rot to the entire bushel. A little compromise, a little false teaching, can undermine the gospel in your mind and heart. As the Galatians discovered, it can even infect and undermine entire churches.

Be on guard against modern-day Judaizers who preach a different gospel than the gospel you have received. Be aware of the techniques these modern-day Judaizers use to appeal to your emotions. Be aware of their use of jargon or warm-and-fuzzy language to create confusion—words such as *inclusive, emergent, harmony, holistic gospel, organic, missional message,* and *contextualization of the gospel.* Notice, too, that modern-day Judaizers reject the clear and plain-spoken vocabulary of God's Word—terms such as *salvation, justification, truth, sound doctrine, false teaching, heresy,* and *apostasy.*

Like the Judaizers of the first century, today's Judaizers would be uncomfortable, if not downright offended, at Paul's statement, "If anyone is preaching to you a gospel contrary to the one you received, let him be accursed." That's too strong! That's intolerant! That's not inclusive!

But it's the truth. Paul had no patience with false teachers, and neither should we.

The Scriptures tell us that Satan can transform himself into an angel of light to fool the nations (2 Corinthians 11:14). In the same way, Satan can make his false religious system appear enlightened, harmonious, and true. Don't be misled. As Paul warns, those who teach a false gospel have been set aside for destruction. They are accursed. They deserve to be condemned to hell, because they lead other souls besides themselves into destruction and condemnation.

Strengthen the foundation of your faith, for as the psalmist said, "if the foundations are destroyed, what can the righteous do?" (Psalm 11:3). Don't let anyone weaken the sure, strong foundation of the gospel. Don't let anyone contaminate the purity of your faith in Christ.

The gospel is Jesus plus nothing, *period*.

2

The Uniqueness of Grace

Galatians 1:10-24

There's an ancient fable about an old man, a boy, and a donkey. They traveled the countryside, going from village to village. As they passed through the first village, the man led the donkey and the boy walked behind. The villagers pointed and called, "Hey, old man! Don't you know what a donkey is for? Why aren't you riding it?" So, to please the people, the old man climbed up and rode on the donkey's back.

Later, they reached the second village. The villagers saw the man riding the donkey, followed by the boy, so they jeered. "Mean old man! Why do you make the boy walk while you enjoy the ride?" So, to please the people, the old man got down from the donkey and let the boy ride.

In time, they reached the third village. The villagers pointed and mocked. "Hey, old man! Are you crazy? There's room on that donkey for two to ride!" So, to please the people, the old man climbed on, and both the man and the boy rode the donkey.

They reached the fourth village, and the villagers shouted in rage, "What kind of cruel monster are you? How can you force that poor donkey to carry two people in the hot sun?"

In his frustration, the old man picked up the donkey and carried the beast on his back with the boy running behind. The moral of the story: If you try to please everybody, you'll end up with a donkey on your back.

Being a people-pleaser is no way to live. The apostle Paul clearly understood this truth. In Galatians 1:10, he asks an important rhetorical question:

> For am I now seeking the approval of man, or of God? Or am I trying to please man? If I were still trying to please man, I would not be a servant of Christ (1:10).

I suggest there are three kinds of people in the world: First, there are the Self-Pleasers. These are the self-centered, self-seeking people in the world. They continually ask, *How will this affect me? How can I benefit from the situation? What's in it for me?* The Self-Pleasers rarely utter a sentence without the word *I* or *me* in it. The whole world revolves around their wants and needs.

Second, there are the People-Pleasers. In their own way, People-Pleasers are as self-seeking as the Self-Pleasers. They are still thinking of themselves, but unlike the Self-Pleasers, their main focus is on being accepted and avoiding rejection by others. They worry obsessively about what other people think of them. They constantly seek approval and compliments. They often seem selfless because they volunteer their time and give of themselves, but they do so because they want people to notice them, approve of them, and praise them.

Constantly striving to please others is an exhausting way to live. People-Pleasers are easily offended. They don't take constructive criticism well, because any criticism feels like rejection to them. You might say, "Here's a better way to do that," but what they hear is, "I don't like the way you did that, and I reject you." That's why People-Pleasers are easily hurt, angered, and offended. They are often sad and miserable people.

Third, there are the God-Pleasers. They have stopped trying to please themselves. They have stopped trying to please others. They have devoted themselves to pleasing the Lord. That's the primary motive for everything they do. The foremost question in the mind of a God-Pleaser is, *What is the will of God? Is the thing I'm about to say or do acceptable to him? If I say or do this thing, will God be glorified?*

I believe the entire human race falls into one of those three categories. So the question we must ask ourselves is: Where am I on this list? Am I a Self-Pleaser, a People-Pleaser, or a God-Pleaser?

The apostle Paul knew where he stood. He knew which category he had chosen. So he wrote to the Galatians, "For am I now seeking the approval of man, or of God? Or am I trying to please man? If I were still trying to please man, I would not be a servant of Christ."

A pack of lies about Paul

Paul wants us to know there is hope for the Self-Pleaser and the People-Pleaser. We don't have to live our lives vainly focused on ourselves. We don't have to remain mired in a swamp of self-centeredness. We don't have to spend all of our energies striving after the approval of others. By the grace of God, we can experience the peace and joy that comes with becoming a God-Pleaser.

The apostle Paul was once a People-Pleaser. Before his conversion to Christ, he had been a self-centered, egotistical, ambitious Pharisee. He had craved the recognition and approval of others. He had hungered for praise and acceptance from the leaders of the Pharisee sect. So Paul understood how the legalistic Judaizers thought, because he had once thought the same way.

But after committing his life to Christ, Paul's motivation was transformed. He no longer lived to please himself or to win the approval of others. He lived to please his Lord. He no longer cared what other people thought of a man named Paul. But he cared intensely what people thought of Jesus.

When these Judaizers invaded the churches of Galatia, their motive was to undermine the truth of the gospel. Their modus operandi was to discredit the messenger—Paul himself. And, of course, false teachers still use these tactics today. Instead of arguing the evidence for the Christian gospel, critics prefer to attack the messenger.

The satanic pattern never varies. Satan is an imitator, not a creator, so he uses the same tired tricks again and again, century after century. Unfortunately, the satanic strategy often works. Judging from Paul's letter, it's clear that the satanic strategy was working in Galatia.

The Judaizers had managed to spread confusion throughout the Galatian churches. These false teachers had persuaded many Christians to go along with their deception. They had convinced many Christians that their false gospel was actually a true reinterpretation of the original gospel. They had taught the Christians in Galatia a lie—and they sold that lie by convincing the Galatians that Paul was trying to be a People-Pleaser.

How could that be? How could anyone think that a man of Paul's courage and boldness could possibly be a People-Pleaser? Here's what the Judaizers accused Paul of: They accused him of wanting to make himself and his Jesus-plus-nothing gospel popular among the Gentiles. They accused him of watering down the gospel and reducing its demands so that he could more easily make converts among the non-Jews. They claimed that Paul was just telling the Gentiles what they wanted to hear. They said that he was leaving out the legalistic demands of their "gospel" in order to make it palatable to Gentile audiences.

It was, of course, a pack of lies. Ironically, these false teachers accused Paul of the very sin that he had been converted out of! It was when Paul was a fire-breathing Pharisee that he was truly a consummate People-Pleaser. That was when he was ambitious to rise in the religious hierarchy, ambitious to be known as the chief persecutor of the Christians, ambitious to receive praise and applause from the Pharisee leaders.

When Paul writes, "If I were still trying to please man, I would not be a servant of Christ," he's saying, in effect, "If I were still trying to please man, I would still be out rounding up Christians, persecuting them and dragging them off to their deaths, while collecting praise and promotions from the Jewish religious hierarchy. If I were still trying to please man, I would still be working my way up the ladder of success. When I converted to Christ, it cost me dearly. I lost my reputation among the Pharisees, I lost my opportunities for promotion, I lost all hope of rising in the ranks of the rabbis, I lost my prestige, I lost my comfort and wealth, I lost my dignity and reputation and secure future. And these false teachers call me a People-Pleaser? How ridiculous!"

The Judaizers accused Paul of being exactly what they were: false teachers, People-Pleasers, boasters and braggarts, servants of the self rather than servants of God. Later, in Galatians 6, we will encounter this description of the Judaizers:

> It is those who want to make a good showing in the flesh who would force you to be circumcised, and only in order that they may not be persecuted for the cross of Christ. For even those who are circumcised do not themselves keep the law, but they desire to have you circumcised that they may boast in your flesh (6:12-13).

Here, Paul makes it clear that the motives of these Judaizers are selfish. They want to "make a good showing in the flesh." In other words, they are putting on appearances. They are persuading the Christians in Galatia to practice the legalistic rites and rituals so that the Jewish religious hierarchy won't persecute them as Christians. They don't even keep the Jewish religious law themselves, but they are teaching the Galatian Christians (who are Gentiles, after all) to keep the Jewish law so that the Judaizers can say, "Don't persecute us! We're the good guys. We even teach *Gentile* Christians to observe the Jewish ceremonial law."

Paul validates his credentials

In verses 11 and 12, Paul offers incontrovertible evidence that he is not a People-Pleaser:

> For I would have you know, brothers, that the gospel that was preached by me is not man's gospel. For I did not receive it from any man, nor was I taught it, but I received it through a revelation of Jesus Christ (1:11-12).

Here Paul says that if he had preached a "gospel" manufactured by human ingenuity, it would have looked like all the other false gospels that were floating around the world. The churches he founded would have looked like all the other false cults that ever existed. Of all the world's religions, Christianity is unique. The Christian message is unlike any other.

What do all of the world's religions (except Christianity) have in common? Simply this: They all teach that you can be saved by your own efforts. They all teach that if you follow certain rules and rituals, if you do certain good works, if you chant the right mantras, if you live the right kind of life, you can make yourself acceptable to God, and you can be saved.

Of all the earth's religions, the Christian faith stands alone in saying, "You cannot do anything to save yourself. You must accept the free gift of God's grace."

This is a hard concept for many people. Our sinful human pride is offended by the idea that we are incapable of saving ourselves. It troubles us to think that only God's mercy and grace can save us. It disturbs us to think that God's own Son had to die in order for us to be saved from our sins. We like to think, *Sure, I've sinned a little— but I haven't done anything so bad that Jesus had to die for me! Couldn't I just do a few good works to balance things out?*

As human beings, we continually want to find a way to give ourselves credit for our own salvation. That was the position of the Judaizers. "Sure," they said, "we acknowledge that Jesus died to save us—but in addition to Jesus, we also need rules and rituals and rigmarole to go through. Jesus did his part to save us. Now we have to do our part in saving ourselves."

When Paul said that the gospel he preached is not man's gospel, but he "received it through a revelation of Jesus Christ" (1:12), he was confronting the Judaizers and their false claims. He was making it clear that the gospel of grace was not some human invention. It came in the form of a revelation straight from Jesus Christ himself.

When Paul looked at the Judaizers, he saw his former self, his pre-Christian self. These false teachers were exactly like Paul used to be before his dramatic conversion on the Damascus Road. They had received their religious instruction from the rabbinic traditions by means of human interpretation of God's Word. Most of the rabbis of that time did not study the Scriptures for themselves, but relied instead on human interpreters of the Scriptures as their authority and guide.

Remember how, in the gospel accounts, the scribes and Pharisees doggedly followed Jesus, questioning him, interrogating him, accusing him of violating their laws and traditions, trying desperately to trip him up and discredit him before the crowds. Again and again, Jesus told them that *their* traditions, *their* interpretations, and all the nitpicky rules and laws *they* had added to the Scriptures had made a mockery of the pure, simple truth of God's Word. The Judaizers were in the same mold as the scribes and Pharisees.

To clear up the confusion in the minds of the Galatian Christians, Paul goes on to validate his credentials by telling his life story:

> For you have heard of my former life in Judaism, how I persecuted the church of God violently and tried to destroy it. And I was advancing in Judaism beyond many of my own age among my people, so extremely zealous was I for the traditions of my fathers. But when he who had set me apart before I was born, and who called me by his grace, was pleased to reveal his Son to me, in order that I might preach him among the Gentiles, I did not immediately consult with anyone; nor did I go up to Jerusalem to those who were apostles before me, but I went away into Arabia, and returned again to Damascus.
>
> Then after three years I went up to Jerusalem to visit Cephas and remained with him fifteen days. But I saw none of the other apostles except James the Lord's brother. (In what I am writing to you, before God, I do not lie!) Then I went into the regions of Syria and Cilicia. And I was still unknown in person to the churches of Judea that are in Christ. They only were hearing it said, "He who used to persecute us is now preaching the faith he once tried to destroy." And they glorified God because of me (1:13-24).

Here Paul writes his spiritual biography. He was ambitious to the point of zealous extremism—and he was on a fast track for success, "advancing in Judaism beyond many of my own age."

But God had a different plan for Paul. He had set Paul apart even before he was born, and called Paul by his grace. On the Damascus Road, God revealed his Son to Paul, brought him to faith in Christ, sent him into Arabia for a time of intense Bible study and spiritual growth, then commissioned him to preach the gospel to the Gentiles. After three years of ministry, Paul spent fifteen days being mentored by Cephas (the apostle Peter); then he went out preaching in the Gentile regions north of Israel, in Syria and Cilicia (in southern Turkey). And all the people who had once feared Paul (or Saul, as he was then known) now praised God because of the transformation in this former persecutor of the faith.

Only after Paul came to Christ did he realize what a People-Pleaser he had been. He thought he was zealous for God. He thought he was self-sacrificing. He thought he was a deeply religious servant of God. Only after his conversion did Paul come to realize that his real motive all along had been to:

- gain favor with men
- receive praise from men
- find acceptance and approval from men
- attain validation from men

Once Paul experienced his soul-shattering encounter with the risen Lord, once he understood what his life and purpose were truly all about, his view of himself was transformed. He no longer needed the approval of men. He was accepted by God. He was approved by the Lord Jesus Christ. What greater validation does anyone need than that?

I can identify with Paul. I can empathize with the old preconversion Saul, the people-pleasing Pharisee. And I can empathize with the new post-conversion Paul, who was content to be accepted and approved by God alone.

From my experience, I can say that people-pleasing is an exhausting task. It leads to discontentment, internal conflict, anxiety, and depression. A People-Pleaser never knows his own mind, because he is constantly trying to figure out who he should be and what he should say in order to please other people.

But the person who lives to please God alone can relax. He is free to be fully himself, to be comfortable in his own skin, to stop worrying about what others think. He can speak freely, truthfully, honestly, transparently, because the only person he has to give an account to is God.

During his earthly ministry, Jesus confronted many religious zealots who were blinded by selfish ambition and the desire to receive praise. Jesus told them that they refused to believe in him because they were People-Pleasers: "How can you believe, when you receive glory from one another and do not seek the glory that comes from the only God?" (John 5:44). Or, as the *New Testament in Modern English* renders Jesus's words, "How on earth can you believe while you are forever looking for each other's approval and not for the glory that comes from the one God?" (PHILLIPS).

As a pastor, I love everybody in my church, but it would be impossible to please everybody in my church. So I don't try. My job is to please one person—Jesus Christ. If I know in my heart that my words and actions are pleasing to him, then I can live with the fact that a few in the church I serve may be displeased now and then. I don't *want* to displease anyone, and I don't *try* to displease anyone. But if my preaching of biblical truth offends anyone, it is only because I am earnestly trying to please my Lord and Master.

One of the unbiblical notions propagated by false preachers today is that God has promised to grant success, health, and wealth to his followers. This "prosperity gospel" is often linked to a promise that if the believer has enough "faith" (demonstrated by donating large sums of money to that preacher's ministry), then God will solve that believer's problems and shower him with success, health, and wealth.

If that principle is true, then all the faithful Christians who were persecuted and martyred in the first century should have been living like kings and queens. Someone should have told those early Christians who were thrown to the lions or burned alive as human torches in Nero's gardens that they should have had more faith, and God would have granted them success, health, and wealth instead of all that needless suffering.

If the prosperity gospel were true, then the apostle Paul should have been a billionaire. But the prosperity gospel is not true. Paul knew he was not promised prosperity, popularity, and a problem-free life in exchange for becoming a Christian. Those who preach this so-called "gospel" are leading people astray just as surely as the Judaizers did in Paul's day.

The false teachers who spread the prosperity gospel are People-Pleasers. They preach a "gospel" that people want to hear—and they preach it at the expense of the gospel of Jesus Christ. Many such gospels are spreading confusion throughout the church today—the prosperity gospel, the "word of faith" or "name-it-and-claim-it" gospel, the universalist "all-roads-lead-to-God" gospel, the social justice gospel, the feminist gospel, the environmentalist gospel, and on and on. And you would be amazed to know how many of these radical gospels actually originated within evangelical circles and institutions.

All of these false gospels are the result of Christians wanting to please people more than they want to please God and remain true to his Word. People pleasing is a deadly virus that spreads quickly in the church, producing spiritual death.

Sin will have no dominion

In Paul's spiritual autobiography, he writes that when God revealed Jesus to him, "I did not immediately consult with anyone; nor did I go up to Jerusalem to those who were apostles before me, but I went away into Arabia." Upon his conversion, Paul lost all his motivation to please others. He didn't go and meet with other leading Christians and say, "I have a wonderful testimony to share." He didn't seek the welcoming approval of the apostles. Instead, he went off alone to Arabia, where he studied and meditated and was instructed by the Lord.

In other words, Paul's conversion changed him from a People-Pleaser to a God-Pleaser. In order to move from self-centered people-pleasing to Christ-centered God-pleasing, you have to comprehend the intervention of God's sovereign grace into your life. If you don't grasp the enormity of God's grace in your life, you won't break free of the cycle of people-pleasing.

The sovereign grace of God, not any effort of our own, calls us out of darkness and into his light. The sovereign grace of God called a persecutor and People-Pleaser named Saul and transformed him into Paul, the selfless apostle of grace. The sovereign grace of God took Simon Peter, the man who had denied Jesus three times, and transformed him into the apostle Peter, who boldly gave himself to be martyred for his Lord. The sovereign and amazing grace of God transformed the hardened heart of a slave trader into the loving, grateful heart of the evangelist and hymn writer John Newton.

The Christian faith is the only faith that teaches that we are saved by grace through faith in Jesus, plus nothing. The Christian faith is unique because the grace of God is unique—no other religion in the world proclaims God's grace. Without the uniqueness of the grace of God, Christianity would be just another cult. It would be a tree without fruit, a well without water, a cloud without rain.

The tragedy of our day is that many people sitting in the pews of our churches don't comprehend the grace of God. The purpose of God's grace is not to excuse the sinner or rationalize sin away. The purpose of God's grace is to justify and transform the sinner.

When Jesus spoke to the woman caught in adultery (John 8:1-11), he didn't say to her, "It's okay, you couldn't help it. You're just a product of your environment. Besides, everybody else is doing it." No, he forgave her, he showed grace to her, and then he said, "Go, and from now on sin no more." That is a proper understanding of grace.

Grace does not pretend that sin doesn't matter. Grace does not pretend that sin is not sin. Grace does not merely spritz perfume on sin to cover up its stench. If the thing we call grace does not produce change and transformation, then it is not the grace of God. In his letter to the Christians in Rome, Paul wrote:

> What shall we say then? Are we to continue in sin that grace may abound? By no means! How can we who died to sin still live in it?…
>
> Let not sin therefore reign in your mortal body, to make you obey its passions…For sin will have no dominion over you, since you are not under law but under grace (Romans 6:1-2,12,14).

For the Christian, sin is a choice. We can choose to reject sin—or we can choose to permit sin to reign in our bodies. We can choose to flee temptation—or we can choose to obey the passions of sin.

Some people say, "I have no choice but to sin." Nonsense! We are all tempted, but we all have free will, the power to choose. And Christians have the power of the Holy Spirit to rely on. Every time you sin, it's because *you made a choice* to sin.

God has called you to a transformed lifestyle. If you refuse to change, that is your choice. If you refuse to change, then you are rejecting the amazing grace of God.

Paul did not choose to be saved, much less to be an apostle. He undoubtedly understood, more than any of us, what it means to be *chosen* by the grace of God. But even though Paul was chosen by God, he still had free will. He still could have rejected God's grace.

In the same way, it is only by the sovereign grace of God that he chose you for salvation, called you into his service, brought you into his kingdom, opened the eyes of your spiritual understanding, predestined you to eternity with him, and adopted you as his child. But even though you were chosen by God, you still have free will. You still have to choose to follow God day by day and hour by hour.

Until you understand these truths, not just as mental concepts but as the life-transforming touchstones of your existence, you will never understand how to move from being self-seeking and people-pleasing to being a God-Pleaser. Once the sovereign grace of God becomes real to you, it will become the lens through which you view all of reality. Through the lens of God's grace you will:

- experience God's joy
- know the serenity of no longer chasing after the approval of others
- live a life of integrity, no longer trying to accommodate the opinions of others
- live a life free from anxiety, worry, and fear
- stop living to make a good impression
- start living to serve Christ

Even in those times when you feel you can't accept yourself, you will rest secure in the knowledge that God has chosen you and accepted you.

The grace of God is unique

Jonathan Edwards was a great theologian and the third president of the College of New Jersey (now known as Princeton University). Edwards was also used by God in a mighty way as one of the leaders of the revival movement known as the Great Awakening.

One of Jonathan Edwards's daughters had a wildly unpredictable and often violent temper. Only those who were closest to daughter Emily ever saw this side of her; to people outside the family, she seemed sweet and pleasant. Her ungovernable temper was a family secret.

One day, a young man came to Jonathan Edwards and asked for Emily's hand in marriage. He was a fine young man from a good family, and he thought that asking Jonathan Edwards for permission would be a mere formality. He was astonished when Edwards replied, "No, you can't marry my daughter."

"But I love her and she loves me," the young man pleaded.

"You can't have her."

"I am well-to-do and I can support her."

"Nevertheless, you can't have her."

"May I ask, sir, if you have heard anything against my character?"

"No, I haven't heard anything against you," Edwards said. "I think you are a promising young man and that's why you can't have her. She's got a very bad temper, and you wouldn't be happy with her."

"Why, Mr. Edwards, I thought Emily was a Christian. She is a Christian, isn't she?"

"Certainly she is. But, young man, when you grow older, you'll be able to understand that there are some folks that the grace of God can live with that you cannot live with."[7]

The grace of God is truly amazing and it is sovereign. The grace of God can even touch the lives of people you and I could never tolerate. You won't find God's grace in Buddhism, Islam, Hinduism,

Taoism, Shintoism, Shamanisn, Gnosticism, Mormonism, Wicca, Baha'i, Unitarianism, or any other *ism* you could name.

The grace of God is unique—and it is unique to the gospel of Jesus Christ.

3

Freedom from Performance

Galatians 2

Galatians is Paul's epistle of Christian liberty, and the concept of Christian liberty speaks to the heart of every freedom-loving American, including this Egyptian-born American. It's a theme Paul wrote about in other letters as well. For example, writing to the church in Corinth, Paul said, "Now the Lord is the Spirit, and where the Spirit of the Lord is, there is freedom" (2 Corinthians 3:17).

Freedom is a precious thing, and we Americans guard our freedom tenaciously. We have fought wars for the sake of freedom. We believe our freedoms come from God, not from government, and that the function of good government is to defend our God-given rights. That's why the Declaration of Independence says, "We hold these truths to be self-evident, that all men are created equal, that they are endowed by their Creator with certain unalienable Rights, that among these are Life, Liberty and the pursuit of Happiness."

Soon after the U.S. Constitution was sent to the states in 1787 for ratification, the founding fathers realized that the Constitution was not complete. Many Americans were uneasy about the new Constitution because, as James Madison observed, "it did not contain effectual provision against encroachments on particular rights."

So the founders began work on a series of amendments, known as the Bill of Rights, to limit the power of government and guarantee the freedom of American citizens—freedom of religion, speech, the press, and assembly; the freedom to petition the government; the right to keep and bear arms; freedom from unreasonable search and seizure; the right to due process and freedom from double jeopardy, self-incrimination, and eminent domain; and on and on.

Today, however, many of us wonder if the Bill of Rights still applies to us anymore. How free are we when grandmothers and children are intimately groped by airport security screeners?[8] When our children are told they can't pray, read the Bible, or wear Christian symbols at school?[9] When our public streets, malls, and campuses are increasingly being monitored by *1984*-style surveillance cameras?[10]

Many of us take freedom for granted, assuming it will always be there and we don't need to do anything to protect it. Few of us realize how many freedoms we've lost over the past few decades as they have been steadily chipped away. Just a few years ago, it would have been unthinkable that government officials would shut down a weekly home Bible study and send the leader to jail (supposedly for zoning reasons).[11] But these attacks on our freedom are becoming more and more common.

People in former Iron Curtain countries now enjoy more freedom than Americans do in these red-tape-tangled times we live in. Someone has suggested that America's motto should be changed from "In God We Trust" to "Do You Have a Permit for That?" Is America still "the land of the free and the home of the brave"?

At the same time we are losing our personal and political freedom, we are also surrendering our social and economic freedom. We choose to live as slaves to conformity, obsessed with wearing the right clothes, living in the right neighborhoods, driving the right car, attending the right events, thinking the thoughts and saying the words that will win the approval of the right people.

And we are surrendering ourselves to debt slavery, economic bondage. We enslave ourselves through spending beyond our means in order to have all the right possessions.

The Ultimate Reality has come

God doesn't want us to live in bondage of any kind. Freedom is at the very heart of the gospel of the Lord Jesus Christ. Here in the book of Galatians, the apostle Paul tells us that one of the chief aims of the false teachers, the Judaizers, was to spy on the freedom enjoyed by the Christians in Galatia. Unfortunately, our human tendency to seek the acceptance and approval of others often leads us to surrender our Christian freedom.

In Galatians 2, Paul continues the spiritual biography that he began in Galatians 1:

> Then after fourteen years I went up again to Jerusalem with Barnabas, taking Titus along with me. I went up because of a revelation and set before them (though privately before those who seemed influential) the gospel that I proclaim among the Gentiles, in order to make sure I was not running or had not run in vain. But even Titus, who was with me, was not forced to be circumcised, though he was a Greek. Yet because of false brothers

secretly brought in—who slipped in to spy out our freedom that we have in Christ Jesus, so that they might bring
us into slavery—to them we did not yield in submission
even for a moment, so that the truth of the gospel might
be preserved for you. And from those who seemed to
be influential (what they were makes no difference to me;
God shows no partiality)—those, I say, who seemed influential added nothing to me. On the contrary, when they
saw that I had been entrusted with the gospel to the uncircumcised, just as Peter had been entrusted with the gospel to the circumcised (for he who worked through Peter
for his apostolic ministry to the circumcised worked also
through me for mine to the Gentiles), and when James
and Cephas and John, who seemed to be pillars, per-
ceived the grace that was given to me, they gave the right
hand of fellowship to Barnabas and me, that we should
go to the Gentiles and they to the circumcised. Only, they
asked us to remember the poor, the very thing I was eager
to do (2:1-10).

Paul received his gospel and his apostleship directly from the
Lord Jesus Christ. His message and commissioning by Jesus were
later affirmed by three "pillars" of the church, the apostle James, the
apostle Peter (Cephas), and the apostle John. These three pillars con-
firmed Paul's gospel, which says that salvation comes through the
grace of the Lord Jesus Christ alone, not through any works of the law.

Christ did not do away with the moral law or invalidate the
moral law. Rather, he *fulfilled* all the moral and ceremonial laws—
and that is why we are free in him. The ceremonial laws were all
symbols that pointed to Jesus, the Ultimate Reality. Once the Reality had come, the symbols no longer needed to be observed. On
the other hand, the moral law (the Ten Commandments) was and
is designed to drive us to Christ.

What does it mean to be free in Christ? It means that not only are we under no obligation to keep the ceremonial law, but the rituals of the law also no longer serve any purpose. Since the only way we can be saved is through faith in the Lord Jesus Christ, it makes absolutely no sense to add the obligations of the ceremonial law to our faith.

Christian freedom is a troubling concept to a legalist. False teachers want to keep people bound up and enslaved and under their control. If you are free, a false teacher can't enslave and control you. The Judaizers, seeing the Christians in Galatia enjoying their freedom in Christ, could not allow that. So they went around spying on the liberty of these Christians. And the reason they spied on Christian liberty was to find a way to destroy that liberty and bring the Galatian believers back into bondage.

So the apostle Paul tenaciously battled these wolves in sheep's clothing. He preached the message he had received directly from the Lord Jesus Christ—the good news of salvation by grace through faith alone in Christ alone. It was the same message that Peter, John, and James received from Jesus, and which they themselves preached. Though Paul received the gospel in a different way than Peter, James, and John did, the message they received was identical.

Disobedience, desire, and dullness

When Paul began telling his spiritual autobiography in Galatians 1, he said that, after his conversion, he went to Arabia for a while, then he returned to Damascus, where he preached the gospel of Jesus Christ for three years. At the end of that three-year period, he went to Jerusalem and visited with Peter for fifteen days. Then he went into the Gentile regions of Syria and Cilicia and preached there for fourteen years before returning once again to Jerusalem.

So, except for a short fifteen-day stay in Jerusalem with Peter early in his ministry, Paul has spent a total of seventeen years from his conversion until his next meeting with Peter, James, and John, the pillars of the church in Jerusalem. In all that time, Paul has had very little opportunity to compare notes with the other disciples—yet his gospel is exactly the same gospel preached by the pillars themselves.

In fact, Paul's understanding of Christian freedom was so clear and doctrinally sound that, on one occasion, he actually had to correct Peter because Peter had gotten off track:

> But when Cephas came to Antioch, I opposed him to his face, because he stood condemned. For before certain men came from James, he was eating with the Gentiles; but when they came he drew back and separated himself, fearing the circumcision party. And the rest of the Jews acted hypocritically along with him, so that even Barnabas was led astray by their hypocrisy. But when I saw that their conduct was not in step with the truth of the gospel, I said to Cephas before them all, "If you, though a Jew, live like a Gentile and not like a Jew, how can you force the Gentiles to live like Jews?" (2:11-14)

Peter had become concerned about what other people might think of him. He had become intimidated by a group of legalistic Judaizers Paul calls "the circumcision party." And because Peter was a leader in the church, many other Jewish Christians were following Peter's lead and behaving the same way, separating themselves from the uncircumcised Gentile believers, as if Gentile Christians were second-class citizens in the church.

Paul's understanding of the gospel and the freedom it brings was so clear in his mind that he instantly recognized Peter's hypocrisy. So Paul confronted the apostle's hypocritical behavior.

We can't be too hard on Peter. This is a pattern that is all too common among even the most mature and committed Christians.

Many Christians start out well. They are in tune with God and his will for their lives. But over time, they begin to lose their sensitivity to the voice of the Shepherd. They start to drift into patterns of thinking and behaving that are inconsistent with the pure, simple truth of the gospel.

Why does this happen? After years of studying this phenomenon, I have come up with three reasons.

The first is *disobedience*. Many Christians begin their spiritual journey with an eagerness to study the Word of God and obey what it says. But time passes and the newness of their spiritual experience begins to wear off. They come across some of the harder commands of Scripture, and suddenly they are not so eager to obey.

We see this principle in the life of King Saul in the Old Testament. In 1 Samuel 10:8, God told Saul (through the prophet Samuel) to wait for divine instructions before going into battle. But Saul got tired of waiting, so he began preparing for battle by usurping the role of a Levite priest and offering the sacrifices himself. Because Saul disobeyed, God removed the kingship from Saul (1 Samuel 13:14). He also disobeyed by failing to destroy the Amalekite nation, sparing their king and keeping the choicest livestock. When King Saul disobeyed God, ran ahead of God, and refused to listen to God's voice, he ceased to be God's man.

When we replace God's commandments with our own made-up religious rules and rituals, our own legalistic add-ons, we have moved from obedience to disobedience—and we have ceased to be faithful servants. God cannot use us if we reject his plan and his will for our lives.

The second reason for spiritual drift is *desire*. Our desires are powerful motivators. Our highest desires are spiritual desires: the desire to serve God and serve others, to share Christ and lead others to salvation, to reach out in compassion to people in need. But we also have desires that come from our sin nature, from the flesh: lust, greed, revenge, gossip, criticism, and more.

As Christians, our goal should be to submit our desires to God's control. This means that we ask God to purify, control, and channel our desires for his service and his glory. If God is not in control of our desires, then our desires will be out of control—and God will not be able to use us.

The story of David and Bathsheba, told in 2 Samuel 11, is the story of a king who allowed his desires to overrule his faithfulness to God and country. "In the spring of the year, the time when kings go out to battle," the Scriptures tell us, David remained behind, idling in his palace while his generals went off to war. He took a walk on the roof of the palace, looked down, and saw the lovely Bathsheba bathing. He desired her, he did not rely on God to control his desire, and the desire began to control him. Ultimately, David ended up committing adultery and murder. He even sabotaged Israel's war effort, killing one of his own generals, in order to cover up his sin. In the end, David paid dearly for his failure to submit his desire to the control of the Lord.

The third reason is *dullness*. There is a progression to these three *D*s. When you are disobedient, and you let your desires control you, the inevitable result is that you lose your spiritual sharpness—and you enter a state of spiritual dullness. You lose your spiritual sensitivity. You become incapable of hearing the voice of the Lord.

At the beginning of Galatians 2, Paul tells us, "Then after fourteen years I went up again to Jerusalem with Barnabas, taking Titus along with me. I went up because of a revelation..." What kind of revelation? A *divine* revelation, a revelation that came directly from God. Throughout his Christian life, throughout his ministry as a preacher and missionary, the apostle Paul continually listened to the voice of God. He was in tune with the revelation of God.

It began when he heard the voice of the Lord on the road to Damascus, and he repented of his sins and allowed God to transform his life. Paul continued listening to the voice of God as he went off to Arabia for a time of Scripture study and meditation, because it was probably during that time of seclusion that Jesus Christ revealed his gospel to Paul. The apostle Paul continued listening to the voice of God as he took the gospel to the Gentile nations.

As you study the life of the apostle Paul, you'll see that, in everything he did and said, he exhibited a faithful obedience to the voice of God. Paul was sensitive to the Lord's direction in his life. He never placed conditions on God's leading. He never said, as we often do, "Lord, I will go anywhere and do anything for you—as long as the price is not too high, as long as the sacrifice is not too great, as long as it doesn't involve going to *that* place, as long as I don't have to do this unpleasant chore or deal with those unpleasant people, as long as I don't have to leave my comfort zone. But Lord, with those few conditions, I am totally willing to go anywhere and do anything for you."

Paul never placed conditions on the leading of the Lord Jesus. He relied on the Holy Spirit and knew that God's plan for him was best. He didn't expect God to consult him when God permitted him to be persecuted or arrested or shipwrecked or beaten or flogged or stoned. His attitude toward God was simply, "I'll go where you send me. I'll do what you command. I'll endure what you decree."

Beware of pseudo-Christians

As Paul told his story to these poor, confused Galatians, he made few references to the false teachers who had spread confusion in the Galatian churches. In essence, he was saying, "It's not worth fighting with these false teachers." In a fight between a bulldog and a skunk, the bulldog would undoubtedly win—but he'd probably conclude that the price of victory was too high.

So Paul related the story of coming to Jerusalem and conferring with Peter, James, and John. The details of this meeting are also related in Acts 15:1-21. When these three pillars heard Paul and Barnabas tell how God was working in the lives of Gentile believers like Titus, they had a clear sense of the grace God had given to Paul. As Paul tells it, the apostles "gave the right hand of fellowship to Barnabas and me, that we should go to the Gentiles and they to the circumcised" (2:9).

The "right hand of fellowship" is an ancient Middle Eastern custom meaning, "we are in agreement." Peter and the other leaders of the church knew that God had called Paul to preach the gospel among the Gentiles, just as Peter had been called to preach the gospel to the Jews.

But the Judaizers were so obsessed with their ceremonies and traditions that they simply would not give up. As Paul describes it, some "false brothers" were secretly brought in to spy and to bring the Christians into slavery to legalism. *The New Testament in Modern English* refers to these "false brothers" as "pseudo-Christians, who wormed their way into our meeting to spy on the liberty we enjoy in Jesus Christ" (2:4 PHILLIPS). These pseudo-Christian false brothers were not Orthodox Jews and they were not liberated Christians. They had created their own hybrid faith, consisting of Jesus *plus* legalistic works.

This hybrid faith still infects the church today. In many churches, if you ask the leaders, "Do you believe in Jesus?" they will answer yes. But you need to ask a lot of follow-up questions in order to understand what they really mean by "believing in Jesus." Here's how the dialogue might go:

Do you believe in Jesus? "Yes."

Do you believe what he said in John 14:6, that he is the only way to heaven and no one comes to the Father but by him? "Well,

I believe Jesus is *one* way to heaven, but not the *only* way. There are many paths, but they all lead to God."

Do you believe that Jesus died and was resurrected? "Yes."

Oh, then you believe his resurrection was a *physical* resurrection from the dead, right? "No thinking person believes in literal miracles. We believe that his influence, his message, his good news emerged from the tomb, but not his physical body."

Do you believe that Jesus is the Son of God? "Yes, we believe that."

Oh, then you believe in his divinity—that Jesus was not only fully man but also fully God, right? "No, when we say that Jesus is the Son of God, we simply mean that we are all sons and daughters of God."

Well, do you believe that the Bible is the inspired Word of God? "Oh, absolutely. The Bible is certainly inspired, no question about it."

So you agree that the Bible is God's infallible and authoritative Word to the human race, right? "Not exactly. When we said that the Bible is inspired, we meant that it is inspired in the same way that Shakespeare's plays are inspired. There are many wonderful insights scattered throughout the Bible."

It can be frustrating trying to carry on a conversation with such people, because they use the same words and phrases you use, but they don't mean the same thing. In fact, their meaning for certain concepts is the *opposite* of the biblical meaning. To call Jesus a "son of God" in the sense that we are all supposedly "children of God" is worse than meaningless—it's an outright lie! The Bible never says that all human beings are "children of God," but only those who have received Christ as Lord and Savior (see John 1:12; 1 John 3:1 and 10).

These Judaizers were much like so many culturally Christian people today. They were not traditional Orthodox Jews, because they claimed to follow Christ. Yet they were not apostolic Christians who believed the teachings of Jesus, Peter, and Paul. They took the basic teachings of Christ, and they added demands that the Christians must keep the ceremonial Jewish law in order to be saved. They served up a tepid stew that claimed to be both Christian and Jewish, but was really neither.

No one is immune

The goal of the Judaizers was to promote legalistic self-righteousness and good works in order to earn favor from God. They rejected grace and canceled out Christ's work upon the cross. Instead of enjoying the rich freedom of God's grace, they chose enslavement to performance in a vain attempt to win God's approval—and they tried to take as many people as possible with them into heresy and error. So Paul makes this blunt reply to the heresy of the Judaizers:

> We ourselves are Jews by birth and not Gentile sinners; yet we know that a person is not justified by works of the law but through faith in Jesus Christ, so we also have believed in Christ Jesus, in order to be justified by faith in Christ and not by works of the law, because by works of the law no one will be justified (2:15-16).

Paul is saying, in effect, "Here I am, a Jew by birth and an heir of the great traditions of the Jewish faith—but you don't see me adding legalistic rules and rituals to my faith. That's because I live by the great truth at the heart of the gospel: salvation is by grace through faith alone—not of works. No one has ever been justified and saved by works of the law, and no one ever will be. The so-called gospel of the Judaizers is a lie. Don't fall for their error."

We're easily tempted to think, *Oh, I could never fall for the error of the Judaizers!* But no one is immune. The great sin of the Judaizers is that they corrupted the pure faith that God had revealed in Jesus Christ. We have seen this error again and again in the Scriptures, from Cain, who wanted to worship God in his own way, to the apostle Peter, who compromised the truth of the gospel for the sake of pleasing others and being accepted by others. If Peter is not immune to this sin, then neither are you and I.

It's a universal temptation, common to all human beings: we tend to base our self-worth on our achievements, our works, the things we have earned and acquired. That is a strategy Satan continually uses against us. If Satan can convince us that God's acceptance of us is based on our performance rather than God's grace, then Satan wins.

Unfortunately, we as Christian parents often convey this misconception to our children. We often condition our children to believe they are accepted based on their performance. In subtle ways, often without realizing it, we communicate to our children that if they don't achieve good grades, if they don't make the team, if they don't perform well in music or in sports, then they are not fully accepted, they are not "good enough." Though we would never say it in so many words, this is the message they hear. As a result, many children grow up with a sense that the only true measure of their self-worth is their performance, their success, and their popularity.

As parents, we frequently communicate to our children that life is all about going to the right schools, playing on the right team, maintaining a certain image, and achieving a certain social status. Our motives may be good. We may be trying to teach our children the importance of a strong work ethic. I know this was my father's goal when he told me, again and again, "You are not worth a dollar unless you can earn a dollar." But the message I received from my father's words was not, "Be motivated, work hard!" The message I heard was, "You are worthless!"—because he usually recited those words when I had demonstrated a lack of initiative.

I grew up with a sense of guilt. I felt like a failure if I wasn't working twenty-five hours a day. I was driven by the fear that I would end up having lived a worthless life, a failure and a disappointment to my father. Only the grace of God and the Lord's deliverance rescued me from the guilt and drivenness I felt because of those words.

Please understand, as with every other aspect of parenting, this is a balancing act. A child who is lazy by nature needs to learn the importance of a strong work ethic and self-discipline. As Paul writes, "If anyone is not willing to work, let him not eat" (2 Thessalonians 3:10). Laziness is a character flaw and industriousness is a virtue that pleases the Lord. Again, Paul writes, "Whatever you do, work heartily, as for the Lord and not for men" (Colossians 3:23).

But we must be careful never to equate laziness with worthlessness. We should never convey to our children that performance equals worth, because that message produces driven adults who never feel they have done enough, and who never enjoy the freedom of God's grace.

The Judaizers tried to inflict a performance-based, legalistic gospel of works, a false gospel that canceled out the grace of God. Paul fought them tooth and nail. Ultimately, the legalistic gospel leads to dishonesty and hypocrisy, because no one can measure up to the demands of the law. Everyone who tries to please God by their legalistic performance ends up faking it, just as the Pharisees and the Judaizers did.

This same principle still operates today. Churches today are filled with people wearing religious masks. When they are with their worldly friends, you would never know that they profess to be Christians. And when they are with their Christian friends, they speak in their evangelical jargon and behave in an oh-so-spiritual way.

They are afraid that their secular friends might find them out as Christians, or that their Christian friends might find them out as hypocrites. They are fearful, inconsistent, and vacillating. It's exhausting to continually have to act and speak as someone you are not.

How do we put an end to this Christian masquerade? How do we stop living as hypocrites and start living as authentic Christians? How do we step out from behind the mask and become who we truly are?

Answer: We must accept our freedom in Christ. We must understand it, live it, revel in it, exult in it, and praise God for it. The only way to live free in Christ is to fully grasp the grace of Jesus Christ.

The law drives us to Christ

For a while, the apostle Peter lost sight of the grace of Jesus Christ. So the apostle Paul had to rebuke Peter—bluntly, publicly, and to his face—for his vacillation and inconsistency. Peter had fallen prey to the performance syndrome. Peter had walked alongside Jesus, had made the great "you are the Christ" profession of faith, had been with Christ on the Mount of Transfiguration—yet he had lost sight of grace. He had fallen into the trap of performance. He had fallen short of his freedom in Christ.

It's shocking to think that Peter succumbed to this error. These Judaizers were not only false Christians, they were not even good Jews. If they had read the Hebrew Scriptures, they would know that, as the prophet Samuel said, "Behold, to obey is better than sacrifice, and to listen than the fat of rams" (1 Samuel 15:22). Or as the prophet Isaiah said:

> "What to me is the multitude of your sacrifices?
>   says the LORD;
> I have had enough of burnt offerings of rams
>   and the fat of well-fed beasts;

I do not delight in the blood of bulls,
    or of lambs, or of goats…

"Wash yourselves; make yourselves clean;
    remove the evil of your deeds from before my eyes;
cease to do evil,
    learn to do good;
seek justice,
    correct oppression;
bring justice to the fatherless,
    plead the widow's cause."

(Isaiah 1:11,16-17)

God is not interested in rituals and rites and sacrifices. All the rituals of the law were for our sake, not his. The symbols were to remind us and teach us what is required in order to purchase our redemption: the shedding of innocent blood. The Judaizers, the Pharisees, and the other legalists fall into the trap of thinking that God is concerned with all of these religious rules and regulations. They fail to understand that God looks upon the heart. He wants us to love him, serve him, and obey him out of a clean and pure heart.

God doesn't care how many hours you spend singing in the choir or teaching Sunday school or serving in the church soup kitchen. He wants to know if you love him, if you love others, if you serve from a grateful heart, if you obey from a loving heart, and if your will is truly submitted to his will. The legalists think God is focused on the symbols; but those who truly belong to God know he is focused on the substance. He cares about the reality of your heart, not the rituals you perform.

As Paul tells the Galatians, "we know that a person is not justified by works of the law but through faith in Jesus Christ, so we also have believed in Christ Jesus, in order to be justified by faith in

Christ and not by works of the law, because by works of the law no one will be justified" (2:16).

No amount of performance can make us righteous, because the root of our sinfulness doesn't lie in our actions but in the fallenness of our hearts. Our most basic problem is not what we *do* but what we *are*. Our sinful actions are only the outward expression of our sinful thoughts. Even if we change our actions, even if we are on our best behavior, we are powerless to change our basic nature.

The law of Moses is a mirror God holds up to our faces to show us what we really are. A mirror cannot cleanse our face. A mirror cannot shave our beard. A mirror cannot comb our hair. It can only show us the truth about ourselves. The law of Moses shows us how sinful we are, but it cannot cleanse us from our sins. Only the blood of Jesus can cleanse us from our unrighteousness.

The function of the law is to drive us to Christ. Once we are cleansed by the blood of Christ, we will think that the mirror is wonderful. But until we are cleansed, all the mirror does is remind us of how wretched and sinful we truly are.

Our identity in Christ

The most destructive effect of legalism is that it undermines the power of the cross. If we can be saved by keeping the law, then why did Jesus have to die on the cross? If we can save ourselves through our own efforts, then what is the cross for? To Paul, the cross was everything:

> But if, in our endeavor to be justified in Christ, we too were found to be sinners, is Christ then a servant of sin? Certainly not! For if I rebuild what I tore down, I prove myself to be a transgressor. For through the law I died to the law, so that I might live to God. I have been crucified with Christ. It is no longer I who live, but Christ who lives

in me. And the life I now live in the flesh I live by faith in the Son of God, who loved me and gave himself for me. I do not nullify the grace of God, for if righteousness were through the law, then Christ died for no purpose (2:17-21).

The key principle in this chapter is found in verse 20: "I have been crucified with Christ. It is no longer I who live, but Christ who lives in me." If we can be saved by doing the works of the law in our own strength, then we are not crucified with Christ. If works can save us, then it is we who live, and Christ does not live in us. Legalism cancels out the cross. As Paul concludes, "if righteousness were through the law, then Christ died for no purpose."

We need to daily remind ourselves of who we are in Christ—not how much we have accomplished by our own efforts, not the status we have achieved, not the possessions we have accumulated, but our identity in Christ. What is our identity? Christ in us! Our old identity is dead. We no longer live. What matters is that Christ lives in us, and we live by faith in him.

That is our identity. That is all that matters, not our performance.

The moment we begin to lapse back into relying on our works, our achievements, or our performance for our identity, we need to *stop*. We need to remind ourselves that anything good we are, and anything good we do, is the result of God's grace. We can take credit for nothing. We don't even live. Everything good in our lives is a result of Christ who lives in us.

Near the end of August 1833, Great Britain enacted the Slavery Abolition Act and abolished slavery throughout the British Empire. In those days before telegraph and radio, transoceanic communications were no faster than the fastest sailing ships. It took seven or eight weeks for a sailing ship to cross the Atlantic from England to the West Indies.

Almost immediately after the Slavery Abolition Act was passed, a British ship set sail for the West Indies with the news. It was late October when that ship finally arrived at its Caribbean destination. While the vessel approached an island port city, the captain stood at the railing and shouted to the hundreds of African slaves who lined the shore, "Free! Free! Free! You're all free!" Hearing the news, the freed slaves cheered and threw off their chains.

The truth is that the slaves had been declared free in late August. For two months, they had labored as slaves even though the Parliament had declared them to be free. They didn't know they were free until the ship arrived from England with the good news.

Many of us are like those slaves. God has declared us free—but we don't know we're free. We continue to live as slaves, toiling under legalism or some other false gospel. It's time to accept the truth about our liberty in Christ. It's time to live as free men and women. It's time to cheer and praise God and throw off our chains.

By God's grace, you have been set free. Don't go back into bondage to dead legalism and performance. Accept the grace God has given you. Revel in the freedom he has purchased for you. Stop trying to live a life that is acceptable to God. Instead, live a life of overflowing gratitude to him for setting you free.

Accept his grace. Let Christ live in you.

4

The Answer to Unfulfilled Needs

Galatians 3:1-14

Imagine you are an islander living in isolation in the South Pacific. All your life, you have lived in the shade of a coconut tree, and you know nothing about the outside world. One day, a trunk washes ashore. You haul it up on the beach, crack it open, and find that it is filled with Christian books and magazines.

You start flipping through the books and magazines. By matching pictures to words, you teach yourself how to read. As you read, you begin to piece together a picture of the world that exists far from your island shores.

If all you knew about the world out there was what you learned from Christian books and magazines, what sort of picture of the world would you get? What would you think Christians think about all day long? What would you think is the focus of the Christian mindset?

I think you would picture Christian culture as a generation of people with many unfulfilled, unmet needs. As an islander, the only needs you've had to focus on are finding food and fresh water. But these Christians! Their water pours from a pipe in the wall. A variety of food is available at all times. They are surrounded by fabulous wealth. What could they possibly need?

Yet they constantly complain of a myriad of needs. They spend untold sums of money on self-help books, seminars, retreats, and conferences. They complain of burnout, breakdowns, midlife crises, stress, boredom, anxiety, poor self-image, obesity, anorexia, sexual dysfunction, and on and on. The more you know about life across the ocean, the better you like living under a coconut palm.

Why do we as Christians murmur and complain about so many "unmet needs"? Why are we, as American Christians who live amid incredible blessing, so quick to sound a sour note of discontent? Who is whispering to us, telling us our lives are boring, meaningless, and unfulfilled?

I can tell you who is behind all of our dissatisfaction and complaining. It's the same old low-bellied, poison-fanged, venom-tongued tempter who has bedeviled us from the beginning of time. This deceiver first came to Eve and whispered to her about her supposed unmet, unfulfilled needs. And she believed him—she bought a lie.

Eve was in a garden of plenty, surrounded by all of that luscious fruit, those fragrant flowers, that warm sunshine, and the bubbling springs of purest water—yet the tempter was able to make Eve believe that she was missing out on something, that the good things in life were passing her by. He convinced her that she was missing out on the best life has to offer, that God was holding out on her. He charmed her and hypnotized her, and even convinced her that God had deceived her!

That tempter's strategy worked brilliantly. If something works, why change it? That's why, in all the thousands of years since the Fall of humanity, Satan, the tempter, has followed the same strategy. To this day, his plan is to make you and me feel dissatisfied and discontented amidst all our blessings. He tempts us to murmur and complain about our unmet needs.

Like Eve, we fall for it. Here in Galatians 3, the apostle Paul shines a light on the trap that Satan has set for us. Paul is angry. He's spitting fire. Let's hear what he has to say—not only to the Galatian Christians, but to you and me:

> O foolish Galatians! Who has bewitched you? (3:1a).

Poor Paul! He has obviously forgotten to read Dale Carnegie's *How to Win Friends and Influence People*. He's not going to win any friends by telling them they are foolish and bewitched. But God has called him to speak the truth, boldly and without compromise, and that is what Paul proceeds to do.

Like so many Christians in our day, the Christians in Galatia were in danger of falling away from God's truth. Like a ship that had slipped its moorings, they were drifting out to sea. When Paul had planted the Galatian churches, he had given them the Word of God, the truth of the gospel. They had received it joyfully. They had begun to walk in the Spirit.

Then these false teachers had come into the church and had enticed them away from the gospel that Paul had taught them. I'm not saying they were necessarily in danger of losing their salvation. But they were blinded to the truth and were being led away by a false gospel. Who knows how far they might have wandered if Paul had not confronted them in this letter?

It's worth noting that the Greek word for "foolish" that Paul uses here is not the same word Jesus used in the Sermon on the Mount when he said, "whoever says, 'You fool!' will be liable to the hell of fire" (Matthew 5:22). The word *fool* that Jesus uses implies mental deficiency and was a very judgmental and insulting word in that culture.

Paul does not transgress against the Lord's warning. Instead, he uses the Greek word *anoētos*, which means "unwise," "lacking in understanding," or "intellectually lazy and careless." He is not telling the Galatian Christians that they are stupid and incapable of understanding. He is telling them they are not living up to their intellectual potential, and they should start using their God-given brainpower more effectively. It's the difference between calling someone an "idiot" versus a loving parent telling a child, "You could get better grades if you'd just apply yourself."

The Galatian Christians were not stupid—they were undiscerning. They were not mentally impaired—but they showed poor judgment. They were not fools—but they had behaved foolishly, allowing the Judaizers to deceive them. Paul had led them to Christ and had taught them that Jesus was sufficient for their salvation—but they had allowed the Judaizers to deceive them into thinking that Jesus was not enough.

The believers in Galatia were behaving foolishly because they had stopped relying on the reasonable and well-attested truth of the gospel. They had allowed themselves to be seduced by slick arguments and their own feelings. They had allowed themselves to be tossed here and there by waves and winds of doctrine, by the craftiness and trickery of men, and by the deceitful scheming of Satan. By letting the Judaizers "bewitch" them, the Galatians were like Eve, fascinated and charmed by deceivers and false doctrine.

When Paul says, "O foolish Galatians! Who has bewitched you?" he chooses his words with care. When we yield ourselves up to false doctrine and spiritual deception, we are allowing ourselves to be seduced by witchcraft, by occult powers, by satanic schemes. When we reject God's truth in favor of emotional arguments, we surrender to witchcraft.

Today, many Christians and churches are surrendering God's truth and subordinating God's unchanging Word to the ever-changing spirit of this dying age. If our culture tells us that the church is behind the times, that the church needs to catch up to the feminist agenda or the homosexual agenda or the progressive agenda, we say, "That's right! We *are* behind the times! If we don't change our doctrines and beliefs to suit the mood of our culture, we'll become irrelevant."

We panic. We feel embarrassed about certain passages of Scripture. We apologize for some of the blunt statements made by the Old Testament prophets, or by the apostle Paul, or by Jesus himself. We stop preaching those embarrassing passages, and we try to pretend they aren't really in the Bible. We major on passages that sound more tolerant, inclusive, and seeker-friendly.

We never go as far as Thomas Jefferson, who actually took scissors and paste, and physically cut up the Bible, removing passages he found disagreeable. But in our own way, we soft-pedal those passages that make us squirm uncomfortably in our pews.

Please heed this warning: When we allow the mood of our culture to edit and revise our understanding of Scripture, we have surrendered to witchcraft! O foolish twenty-first-century Christians in America, who has bewitched you?

Abraham's true descendants

Paul goes on to contrast the faith that the Galatian Christians originally received versus the error of the Judaizers that they have begun to embrace:

> It was before your eyes that Jesus Christ was publicly portrayed as crucified. Let me ask you only this: Did you

receive the Spirit by works of the law or by hearing with faith? Are you so foolish? Having begun by the Spirit, are you now being perfected by the flesh? Did you suffer so many things in vain—if indeed it was in vain? Does he who supplies the Spirit to you and works miracles among you do so by works of the law, or by hearing with faith—just as Abraham "believed God, and it was counted to him as righteousness"?

Know then that it is those of faith who are the sons of Abraham. And the Scripture, foreseeing that God would justify the Gentiles by faith, preached the gospel before-hand to Abraham, saying, "In you shall all the nations be blessed." So then, those who are of faith are blessed along with Abraham, the man of faith.

For all who rely on works of the law are under a curse; for it is written, "Cursed be everyone who does not abide by all things written in the Book of the Law, and do them." Now it is evident that no one is justified before God by the law, for "The righteous shall live by faith." But the law is not of faith, rather "The one who does them shall live by them." Christ redeemed us from the curse of the law by becom-ing a curse for us—for it is written, "Cursed is everyone who is hanged on a tree"—so that in Christ Jesus the bless-ing of Abraham might come to the Gentiles, so that we might receive the promised Spirit through faith (3:1b-14).

In other words, Paul is telling the Galatian Christians, "Do you remember what the Spirit of God accomplished in your life when you trusted Jesus for your salvation? Do you remember how you sincerely believed and trusted that your salvation was a gift of God's grace? Do you remember how you simply reached out and accepted this gracious gift, as a penniless beggar receives alms? You didn't work for it. You didn't do anything in your own flesh to perfect the gift of salvation."

Then Paul reminded them of the work of the Holy Spirit in their midst. He said, in effect, "Do you remember how the Holy Spirit came upon you, opened your spiritual eyes, and removed the blinding scales of doubt and unbelief? If your faith in Christ began through the Holy Spirit, why are you trying to perfect it through works of the flesh?"

The presence of the Holy Spirit in the lives of these Galatian Christians was the greatest proof they could have that God had lovingly guaranteed their future in eternity with Christ. The witness of the Holy Spirit was the greatest proof they could have that this faith would carry them through life, through the storms and fires, ups and downs, joys and sorrows, sickness and health, wealth and poverty of this life. Why, then, were they willing to turn their backs on all of that?

In another letter, Paul reminded the believers in Ephesus, "In him you also, when you heard the word of truth, the gospel of your salvation, and believed in him, were sealed with the promised Holy Spirit, who is the guarantee of our inheritance until we acquire possession of it, to the praise of his glory" (Ephesians 1:13-14).

Here in Galatians, Paul makes a parallel observation: "Does he who supplies the Spirit to you and work miracles among you do so by works of the law, or by hearing with faith—just as Abraham 'believed God, and it was counted to him as righteousness'?" (3:5-6). Paul's point is that in both Old Testament times and New Testament times, salvation has always been a gift of God's grace, received by faith, sealed and guaranteed by the Holy Spirit. No one in the history of the human race has ever been saved by keeping the law.

When we were born again by the Spirit, we were sealed by the Spirit. From that moment forward, all we ever had to do for the rest of our lives was to constantly live by the Spirit, walk in the Spirit, and be filled with the Spirit.

Some people think that the Holy Spirit is a goal that we strive for in the Christian life. But Paul tells us, No! The Spirit is not the goal but the source of the Christian life. The Spirit is the reason we believe. Without the Holy Spirit, faith would be impossible.

Others think that the presence of the Holy Spirit in our lives is a by-product of living faithfully for Christ. But Paul tells us, No! The Spirit is the power behind our faithfulness to God. The Spirit is the reason we remain true to God. Without the Holy Spirit, faithfulness would be impossible, and we would fall away from the Lord.

We tend to think that we came to faith in Christ purely of our own volition, our own free will. And while it is true that God did create us with the ability to choose, it is equally true that we would never choose God unless we were brought to faith by the Holy Spirit. We freely chose to accept Christ as our Lord and Savior—yet the Holy Spirit chose us, led us, taught us, and opened the eyes of our understanding so that we could make that choice. This is a paradox, a mystery that our limited human intellects are incapable of solving.

The Holy Spirit was there at the very beginning of our faith experience. The Spirit drew us and taught us and led us to a place of faith and submission to Christ. And as we continue to learn from the Spirit and grow in the Spirit and be filled with the Spirit, our submission to the Holy Spirit will lead us into deeper depths and higher heights of living in him.

The great irony of legalism is that when you try to please God by the works of the flesh, by observing all the legalistic dos and don'ts, by keeping all the religious rules and rituals—God will be far from pleased! But if you serve the Lord in the power of his Holy Spirit, everything you do will find favor in his sight.

Paul reminds us that Abraham "believed God, and it was counted to him as righteousness." Abraham was not saved by the outward act of circumcision, as many legalists believe. He was saved by faith.

His circumcision was merely an outward sign of his inward faith and obedience.

If we think about it for a moment, it becomes obvious that Abraham could not possibly have been saved by the law. For one thing, the law was not given until five hundred years after Abraham. He was saved by grace, not works. He was righteous because he took God at his word. And ever since Abraham, every human being who has lived by faith, who has taken God at his word, has become one of Abraham's true descendants.

What faith is—and is not

When you worship, please don't make the mistake of focusing on the form, the externals, the outward expression, the symbolism. Don't make the mistake of thinking that it is baptism or communion or the Lord's Prayer or the Apostles Creed or standing up or kneeling down or jumping in the aisles that saves you.

When you worship, focus on praise, focus on thankfulness, focus on prayer, focus on singing with a heart full of joy, focus on obedience, focus on God. Let your faith and trust in him be sincere. Let your obedience to him flow from a heart of love and gratitude. Let your praise to him flow from a sense of awe and wonder.

Salvation by grace through faith is not a new concept that Jesus introduced in the New Testament. It's the only plan God has ever had for saving fallen human beings from sin. God never told Israel that the outward act of circumcision would save them. He never told Israel that sacrifices and ceremonies would save them. In fact, God made it clear that these symbols were intended only as an outward sign of an inward faith in God.

That's why God told Israel, "Circumcise therefore the foreskin of your heart, and be no longer stubborn. For the LORD your God is God of gods and Lord of lords, the great, the mighty, and the awesome God, who is not partial and takes no bribe" (Deuteronomy 10:16-17). And that's why God also told Israel, "the righteous shall live by his faith" (Habakkuk 2:4b).

Legalism is an attempt to bribe God with outward displays of religious activity. But God sees through all our pathetic and hypocritical attempts to win his approval through legalism. He looks on the heart, and he knows if our hearts are truly circumcised or not. He knows if we truly love him or not. He knows if we trust him, obey him, and worship him in spirit and in truth.

When you truly understand what it means to have faith in God, you will experience victory in the Christian life. If you are experiencing defeat as a Christian, it is probably because you have failed to understand and apply what it means to have faith.

Genuine faith is the answer to all our anxiety and fear. It's the answer to all our discontentment and dissatisfaction. It's the answer to all our unfulfilled and unmet needs. It's the answer to the sin and wickedness of this world.

As the apostle John has written under the inspiration of the Holy Spirit, "For everyone who has been born of God overcomes the world. And this is the victory that has overcome the world—our faith" (1 John 5:4). And the writer of Hebrews reminds us, "And without faith it is impossible to please him, for whoever would draw near to God must believe that he exists and that he rewards those who seek him" (Hebrews 11:6).

By faith, kingdoms were subdued, righteousness was wrought, promises were fulfilled, the mouths of lions were shut, the hungry were fed, the sick were healed, the weak were made strong, and the armies of the enemy were confounded, confused, and defeated.

Where does faith come from? Paul replies, "So faith comes from hearing, and hearing through the word of Christ" (Romans 10:17). So if you are suffering from burnout, midlife crisis, stress, boredom, anxiety, poor self-image, or the spiritual blahs, don't waste your time and money on self-help books and seminars. Invest in a stronger faith. Go deeper into the Word of God. Let God's thoughts saturate your mind, soak into your soul, and fill your spirit to overflowing.

You don't need to perform mental gymnastics to grow stronger in your faith. You don't have to rev up your emotions to grow stronger in your faith. You don't even have to feel good to be strong in your faith. Faith has nothing to do with feelings. Your feelings can change with the weather, the stock market, a phone call or email, or changing hormones and body chemistry. Never let your mood determine the level of your faith.

Faith has nothing to do with your circumstances. Faith is a certainty and an assurance of God's presence and goodness in our lives—an assurance that looks beyond our circumstances. As the Scriptures tell us, "Now faith is the assurance of things hoped for, the conviction of things not seen" (Hebrews 11:1).

Faith is not believing that God can. Faith is not even believing that God will. Faith is seeing that *God has already done it*. Faith comes from an absolute, unwavering, unbending trust in the infallible Word of God.

Covered by grace—not by a fig leaf

The Judaizers in Galatia were like many legalistic Jews at that time—and like many legalistic Christians of our day. They had reversed the relationship between symbol and substance, between ritual and reality, between circumcision and salvation. The substance and the salvation are the result of God's grace. The symbols and rituals are merely outward manifestations of a change within.

Never confuse the ritual with the reality. Never confuse the symbol with the substance. In Genesis 17:1-14, we read the account of how God gave the covenant and symbol of circumcision to

Abraham. But God did not give Abraham this symbol until fourteen years after God declared Abraham righteous because of his faith (see Genesis 15:6). The reality of Abraham's faith came first; the symbol of circumcision came later.

This is always the biblical pattern. Yet human beings, in their desire to create their own religion instead of obeying God, insist on putting ritual ahead of reality. This kind of do-it-yourself religion is still very much with us today.

The Christian landscape is dotted with churches that have put symbols and rituals ahead of repentance and faith. Millions of people think that because they are third- or fourth-generation Presbyterians or Episcopalians or Catholics, they are Christians. But the truth is that God has only sons and daughters—he doesn't have any grandchildren. You can learn about Jesus from your mom and dad, but you can't inherit Christianity from them.

In Romans, Paul writes, "not all are children of Abraham because they are his offspring...it is not the children of the flesh who are the children of God, but the children of the promise are counted as offspring" (Romans 9:7,8). The true descendants of Abraham are those who follow in the faith of Abraham. Abraham believed and trusted God fully, and God accounted Abraham's faith as righteousness (Genesis 15:6).

God told Abraham to leave home and go to an unknown land, and by faith, Abraham obeyed. God told Abraham to sacrifice his only son, Isaac, through whom God had promised Abraham many descendants. Even though God's command defied logic and broke Abraham's heart, Abraham trusted God and obeyed him and would have sacrificed Isaac if the angel of the Lord had not stopped him. Abraham knew that God would fulfill his promise—even if God had to resurrect Isaac from the dead (Hebrews 11:17-19).

The ancient scribes and teachers of the law taught that salvation comes from keeping the law, yet they had to ignore their own Scriptures to make that claim. As Deuteronomy 27:26 plainly teaches, "'Cursed be anyone who does not confirm the words of this law by doing them.' And all the people shall say, 'Amen.'" In other words, in order to be saved by the law, you have to be morally perfect. You cannot break the law at any time, to even the slightest degree, not even once. Fail just one time—and you are cursed, just as if you had broken the law a thousand times.

The Old Testament legalists, upon reading that verse, should have understood that if the standard is absolute moral perfection, then no one can be saved. Imagine pulling a car up the hill with a tow chain. If just one of the links in the chain breaks, it doesn't matter that all the other links in the chain held fast. All that matters is that one link broke, and that car is going back down the hill, out of control.

If the Old Testament legalists had studied the Scriptures more carefully, they would have seen that Abraham was accounted righteous by God by his faith, not by keeping the law. They would have read the Psalms, and they would have seen that when God was angry with Israel, it was because the people rejected salvation by faith, as the psalmist writes:

> Therefore, when the LORD heard, he was full of wrath;
>> a fire was kindled against Jacob;
>> his anger rose against Israel,
> because they did not believe in God
>> and did not trust his saving power.
>
> (Psalm 78:21-22)

Throughout the Old Testament, we see that salvation is always a work of God's grace, never a result of human effort or religious ritual. After the Fall, Adam and Eve tried to cover themselves with fig leaves—a symbol of human efforts to deal with the sin problem. God, in his grace and mercy, clothed them in animal skins—evidence of the first animal sacrifices, which pointed to the ultimate sacrifice of Jesus Christ (see Genesis 3:21). The sin of Adam and Eve was covered by God's grace, not by the pathetic fig leaf of human effort.

If you are trying to be accepted by God through any other way than the blood of Jesus Christ, you are merely covering yourself with a fig leaf. Your efforts are hopeless and pathetic. Your legalism is bondage to a false religion. You are still lost. You need a Savior.

Don't be taken in by Satan's strategy. He tempts us to focus on the extraneous things in the Christian life, the symbols instead of the substance, the unfulfilled and unmet needs instead of Jesus, the all-sufficient Answer to all of our needs.

Many Christians today suffer from what I call "The Scarlett O'Hara Syndrome." You are probably familiar with Scarlett O'Hara from the novel *Gone with the Wind* by Margaret Mitchell, or the Clark Gable–Vivien Leigh film of the same name. Scarlett, the heroine of the story, was a Southern belle born into wealth and privilege. She had everything a young woman could want—beauty, youth, health, wealth, power, servants, and love. But no matter how much she had, she was never satisfied. She always craved more.

Even though she already possessed the love of Rhett Butler, she desired Ashley Wilkes, the husband of her friend Melanie. She could never be content with what she had, and her lack of contentment drove Rhett Butler to drink—and finally drove him to leave her. When Scarlett finally realize that her husband, Rhett, was the man she really wanted, it was too late. By spending so many years chasing fantasies, Scarlet lost the real love she had once possessed.

We look at the story of this woman and we think, *How foolish and blind she was!* But aren't we guilty of the same foolishness? Don't we easily become restless, wanting more in our spiritual lives than Jesus alone? We have so much, both materially and spiritually, yet we whine and complain about our unmet needs. We claim to be burned out, stressed out, anxious, depressed, and defeated, yet we are just spoiled spiritual Scarletts who don't appreciate all we have in Jesus. We don't appreciate the grace, forgiveness, power, encouragement, and presence of God in our lives.

This is how Satan works. This is how Satan schemes against us and plots our spiritual destruction. He tempts us to focus on our "unmet needs," and to lose sight of all that is ours in Christ.

Don't be misled by Satan. Instead, take authority over the enemy and tell him, "Jesus alone is all I want and all I need!"

And that will be enough.

5

The Long Arm of the Law

Galatians 3:15-29

Tommy's mother had just baked a chocolate cake. The rich aroma was almost more than little Tommy could stand. He salivated as he watched his mother cover the cake with double-fudge frosting.

"When are we going to eat the cake, Mom?" he asked.

"I'm sorry, Tommy," she replied. "That cake is not for us. I'm saving it for the coffee and dessert party tonight. I'm going upstairs to take a nap, so don't touch the cake."

I don't know why Tommy's mother couldn't foresee what would happen next because you and I know! There was Tommy, sitting in a chair, staring at the cake, savoring the aroma, and listening to his stomach growl. He inched his chair a little closer to the cake, merely to admire his mother's handiwork.

He noticed a slight imperfection in the frosting, a little swirl that was not as smooth as it should be. *Mom would want the cake to be perfect*, he reasoned. So he reached out and smoothed the swirl with his finger. Then, of course, he had to lick the frosting off his finger.

He noticed another imperfection on the other side of the cake. *Mom told me not to touch the cake*, he said to himself, *but what she really meant was that I shouldn't eat it. And I'm not really eating it—I'm just making repairs.*

So Tommy tried to smooth out the frosting with his finger, then he licked his finger. He continued turning the cake, looking for imperfections—and finding them. Soon, however, the cake looked worse than when he began his repairs.

Well, Tommy reasoned, *I'm already in this much trouble. I might as well enjoy a piece of cake.*

Tommy was on his second piece of cake when he was startled by his mother's voice, shouting, "Tommy! Didn't I tell you not to touch that cake!"

From Tommy's perspective, his mother was being completely unreasonable. After all, he had used a perfectly logical chain of reasoning to justify two pieces of cake. But all of Tommy's rationalizations failed to address one simple fact: his mother had told him not to touch the cake.

And Tommy had touched the cake.

That is the nature of the law. It is absolute. We cannot circumvent or rationalize away the long arm of the law. We may think we can find a way around the law, but if we break it, we are left without excuse—just like Tommy.

There is only one way we can escape the unrelenting justice and penalty of God's law, and that is by embracing and receiving God's grace.

God has not changed his mind about salvation

Many people, including many Christians, are confused about what it means to be saved. Are we saved by grace or are we saved by keeping the law? Paul addresses this question with an analogy:

> To give a human example, brothers: even with a man-made covenant, no one annuls it or adds to it once it has been ratified. Now the promises were made to Abraham and to his offspring. It does not say, "And to offsprings," referring to many, but referring to one, "And to your offspring," who is Christ. This is what I mean: the law, which came 430 years afterward, does not annul a covenant previously ratified by God, so as to make the promise void. For if the inheritance comes by the law, it no longer comes by promise; but God gave it to Abraham by a promise (3:15-18).

Paul compares the law of Moses to a legal document, drawn up by lawyers, to illustrate the difference between the covenant of grace, which was first given to Abraham, and the law, which was given 430 years later through Moses. Paul has made an intense study of God's covenant with Abraham, and he has noticed something that all the other scribes and teachers of the law seem to have missed. It centers around the word *offspring*.

For centuries, Hebrew scholars had understood *offspring* (or *seed*, as some versions translate the word) to be a *collective noun*—a noun that is singular in form but refers collectively to an entire group of people, Abraham's descendants. But Paul, under the inspiration of the Holy Spirit, noticed that *offspring* can also be understood as a *singular noun*—a reference to one person, not many. If God made promises to Abraham and his singular offspring, who would that offspring be?

The answer, of course, is Jesus the Messiah.

If you view *offspring* as a collective noun, then the people of the nation of Israel were (collectively) the heirs of God's covenant with Abraham. Therefore, in order to be a recipient of God's promise to Abraham, you would have to belong to the nation of Israel. Under Paul's singular noun interpretation of *offspring*, God made the covenant with Abraham and with Abraham's singular offspring, Jesus. So you no longer have to be a member of the Jewish nation in order to receive the promise of God's covenant with Abraham. Instead, you must be in Christ.

How does a person come to be "in Christ"? By grace through faith. Salvation is not a matter of ethnic identity. It's a matter of placing our trust in Jesus Christ as Lord and Savior, in accordance with the promise of God. His promise is irrevocable and unchangeable. His promise cannot be added to or subtracted from.

Abraham received this promise by faith when he believed and trusted in God. The Lord, in accordance with his promise, accounted Abraham's faith as righteousness (Genesis 15:6). Salvation was always by grace through faith, and when the law was given to Moses, 430 years after Abraham received the covenant, the law did not change the covenant. The law did not nullify God's grace or God's plan of salvation.

One thing the law did was create a division between Jews and Gentiles. But Jesus the Messiah, the heir of God's covenant with Abraham, healed that division. By the covenant of grace, Christ brings Jews and Gentiles together in unity and harmony (Ephesians 2:11-18).

No one can be saved by keeping the Ten Commandments because no one can keep them perfectly. Jesus is the only human being who has ever kept the law perfectly, all the time, throughout his life, and he is the only one through whom we can obtain salvation. He is the singular offspring of Abraham who makes the promise of the covenant available to all of humanity.

All of us who are saved by grace through faith in Jesus Christ are now descendants of Abraham. Our faith is accounted to us as righteousness, just as Abraham was justified in the sight of God by faith alone.

The law was of no use whatsoever to Abraham because it was not given until four centuries after he lived. He never even heard of the law. Abraham lived by God's promise, not by the law. And in all the centuries that have come and gone since Abraham walked the earth, God has not changed his mind about the way of salvation.

Nothing less than perfection

Every promise given to Abraham was fulfilled in Jesus Christ and *only* in Christ. The only way anyone can participate in the blessings promised to Abraham is to be a fellow heir with Christ through faith in him.

Before Jesus the Messiah came to earth, salvation was possible only on the basis of looking forward to the cross and anticipating it by faith. After Jesus came, salvation is possible only by looking back to the same cross and receiving Jesus by faith. There has never been a way of salvation apart from the finished work of Christ. And there never will be a different way of salvation.

That's why Jesus said, "I am the way, and the truth, and the life. No one comes to the Father except through me" (John 14:6).

Paul says that, while the promise was given directly to Abraham, the law was given to angels, who in turn gave it to Moses. Why was the law given if it has no power to save us? Good question! Paul gives us the answer:

> Why then the law? It was added because of transgressions, until the offspring should come to whom the promise had been made, and it was put in place through angels by an intermediary. Now an intermediary implies more than one, but God is one.
>
> Is the law then contrary to the promises of God? Certainly not! For if a law had been given that could give life,

then righteousness would indeed be by the law. But the Scripture imprisoned everything under sin, so that the promise by faith in Jesus Christ might be given to those who believe (3:19-22).

The law, Paul says, "was added because of transgressions." In other words, God gave us the law to reveal the total sinfulness of humanity. He gave it to us to demonstrate our utter inability to please God by our works. He gave it to us to show us our absolute need for grace and mercy. He gave it to us to prove to us how much we have rebelled against God.

God gave us the law to confront us with our desperate guilt—and to drive us to the Deliverer. He gave us the law to prove to us that it is impossible for any fallen human being to meet its demands, because the law demands *nothing less than perfection*.

Though we know that no one can be saved by the law, we still uphold God's law to our society—a society that seems to be hurtling at lightning speed toward suicide. We hold up the law of God to our culture so that men and women will see, as if in a mirror, their own sinfulness. We hold up the law of God so that they will see they are violating God's standards of righteous. We hold up the law of God so that they will know they are under divine judgment.

God so loved the world that he gave his only Son—but he also loved the world so much that he gave the law in order to drive men and women to his Son, their Deliverer. The grace of God is meaningless to the one who feels no inadequacy, no need of help. The grace of God is meaningless to the one who doesn't even know he is lost. The grace of God is meaningless to those who feel no need for forgiveness, who don't even know they have offended a holy God. Those who are unaware that they are under God's wrath feel no need to seek God's mercy.

So God, in his compassion and grace, gave us the law to drive men and women to despair over their sins. He gave us the law to stir in us a hunger for salvation, which can be obtained only by grace through faith in the Lord Jesus Christ. God did not give us the law to save us but to drive us to the One who can save us. He gave us the law to move us to grace.

One of the great tragedies of our society is that so many forces in our culture are fighting to eliminate God's law from the landscape. Organizations such as the American Civil Liberties Union (ACLU) and the Freedom from Religion Foundation are filing lawsuit after lawsuit to remove displays of the Ten Commandments from public view. At the same time, sociologists and psychologists are trying to salve people's guilt and anesthetize them to the reality of sin.

For example, when a woman with an unwanted pregnancy goes to Planned Parenthood for counseling, what does she hear? "Don't feel bad. You have nothing to feel guilty about." Of course, the abortion mills have a profit motive for numbing the guilt feelings of their clients. Randy Alcorn, founder of Eternal Perspective Ministries, explains:

> It's counterproductive to try to eliminate guilt feelings without dealing with guilt's cause. Others may say, "You have nothing to feel guilty about," but you know better… You need a permanent solution to your guilt problem, a solution based on reality, not pretense…
>
> The good news is that God loves you and desires to forgive you for your abortion, whether or not you knew what you were doing. But before the good news can be appreciated, we must know the bad news. The bad news is there's true moral guilt, and all of us are guilty of many moral offenses against God, of which abortion is only

one. "All have sinned and fall short of the glory of God" (Romans 3:23).[12]

The law of God is the bad news. It drives us to the good news, which is the grace of God, revealed in Jesus Christ.

When I say that the law is "bad news," I'm not saying that the law is bad. As Paul writes in Romans 7:12, "So the law is holy, and the commandment is holy and righteous and good." The only reason the law is bad news is that we cannot live up to it. As Paul goes on to tell us in Galatians, "Is the law then contrary to the promises of God? Certainly not! For if a law had been given that could give life, then righteousness would indeed be by the law. But the Scripture imprisoned everything under sin, so that the promise by faith in Jesus Christ might be given to those who believe" (3:21-22).

The law is inferior to the promise because the promise saves, the law does not. The promise imparts life, the law does not. The law of God is holy and righteous, but it cannot save us. It was never designed to save us.

Think of the law as the cart and the promise as the horse. The cart is fine, and you can sit in it. The cart is perfectly suited for its purpose. But without the horse, the cart can't take you anywhere. It was never designed to take you anywhere apart from the horse.

The law of God is good, holy, and righteous—but without the promise, without grace, the law can't take you to God. It can't save you. It can do nothing for you. Paul tells us that the law is like a prison cell. It imprisons everything under sin. But salvation by grace through faith in Jesus Christ is the key that unlocks the prison cell.

Don't be outwitted by Satan

In another letter, Paul tells us that, before his conversion to Christ, he was a model Jew, the epitome of legalistic self-righteousness and national pride. He described himself as "circumcised on the eighth day, of the people of Israel, of the tribe of Benjamin, a Hebrew of Hebrews; as to the law, a Pharisee; as to zeal, a persecutor of the church; as to righteousness under the law, blameless" (Philippians 3:5-6). But after experiencing the grace of God, Paul could say:

> But whatever gain I had, I counted as loss for the sake of Christ. Indeed, I count everything as loss because of the surpassing worth of knowing Christ Jesus my Lord. For his sake I have suffered the loss of all things and count them as rubbish, in order that I may gain Christ and be found in him, not having a righteousness of my own that comes from the law, but that which comes through faith in Christ, the righteousness from God that depends on faith (Philippians 3:7-9).

If it were humanly possible to be made righteous by observing the law and keeping the commandments, Paul would have been a supremely righteous man. He was a Hebrew's Hebrew, a Pharisee's Pharisee. It took a lightning bolt from God to penetrate his self-righteousness and shatter his pride.

Paul goes on in Galatians 3 to describe how legalism—depending on the law for salvation—holds people captive:

> Now before faith came, we were held captive under the law, imprisoned until the coming faith would be revealed. So then, the law was our guardian until Christ came, in order that we might be justified by faith. But now that faith has come, we are no longer under a guardian, for in Christ Jesus you are all sons of God, through faith. For as many of you as were baptized into Christ have put on Christ. There is neither Jew nor Greek, there is neither slave nor free, there is no male and female, for you are all one in Christ Jesus. And if you are Christ's, then you are Abraham's offspring, heirs according to promise (3:23-29).

Here Paul discloses another function of the law: "the law was our guardian until Christ came, in order that we might be justified by faith." This word translated *guardian* has a very special meaning in that first-century culture. Some translations have rendered that word *schoolmaster*, but that is not an accurate translation.

In the ancient Greek and Roman world, well-to-do families employed a trustworthy slave who had the duty of supervising the young boys in the family on behalf of their parents. These slaves were guardians. They took the boys to school, made sure that they did their homework, tutored them as necessary, trained them in obedience, and yes, administered discipline, including scoldings and corporal punishment.

The original Greek word Paul uses was *paidagōgos*, from which we get the English word *pedagogue*. Every first-century Galatian reading these verses would immediately understand the point Paul was making: The *paidagōgos* or guardian did not hold a permanent position. His job was temporary, and he was there to oversee the boy's education only until that boy achieved adulthood. Once the boy became an adult, the student-guardian relationship changed. The *paidagōgos* was no longer the master, but now became a friend.

Paul's point is clear. The law is our *paidagōgos*, our master, and it holds us imprisoned until faith in Christ is revealed. The law's function is temporary: God has appointed the law to be our *paidagōgos* to lead us to Christ.

Now, perhaps, you can understand why the law of God has been removed from the halls of government, the halls of education, and the courtrooms of our land. Now you can understand why Satan's unwitting dupes in organizations such as the ACLU and the Freedom from Religion Foundation cry foul and file a lawsuit anytime Christians try to remind the public and the government of God's laws and standards.

These anti-God organizations and individuals like to identify themselves as "freethinkers" or "rationalists" or "brights" or
"humanists." The arrogance of such labels is unmistakable. They
have convinced themselves that their ungodly position is the only
view a rational, intelligent human being could possibly entertain.
They laugh behind their sleeves at these poor, ignorant, supersti-
tious Christians and their ridiculous myths. They have formed an
unholy alliance for the purpose of eradicating God's law from public
life, from the government, from our schools, from our courtrooms,
from our media, and from the arena of commerce and business.

Why are they so rabidly, fanatically, irrationally opposed to
even a nonsectarian display of the Ten Commandments in a public place? Because the law of God creates an awareness of authentic
guilt and sin, and that awareness drives men and women to Jesus
Christ. These people do not want to see others come to Jesus Christ.
And above all, Satan—who quietly inspires their ungodly activism—
does not want to see men and women come to Christ.

Don't be outwitted by Satan. Don't be ignorant of his schemes.
Satan works hard with his human coconspirators (though most of
them are completely unaware of his existence) to keep men and
women from realizing their need of a Savior. On almost any given
day, you can open your newspaper and see Satan at work, trying to
hide God's law from the eyes of men and women.

Whenever you see a lawsuit filed against a display of the Ten
Commandments, don't assume that the real villain in that story is
made of flesh and blood. Remember what Paul told the Christians
in Ephesus: "For we do not wrestle against flesh and blood, but
against the rulers, against the authorities, against the cosmic powers over this present darkness, against the spiritual forces of evil in
the heavenly places" (Ephesians 6:12).

And yes, we can actually see evidence daily of that cosmic battle being waged in courtrooms and in newspaper headlines. It is a war to erase God's law from the landscape of our culture—a battle to keep men and women from finding their way to the grace of God and faith in the Lord Jesus Christ.

A pipeline to God's grace

A story is told about T.E. Lawrence, the British army officer who aided the Arab Revolt against the Ottoman Empire and gained fame as "Lawrence of Arabia." After World War I, Lawrence led a delegation of Arabs from Saudi Arabia to the Paris Peace Conference of 1919.

When the men from Arabia were shown to their hotel rooms, they were amazed to discover that they could turn a knob in the bathroom and the bathtub would magically fill with water from a spigot in the wall. In Arabia, water was a precious commodity that had to be drawn from a well and used sparingly. It was a shock to see water dispensed so easily and lavishly.

After the conference, as the delegation prepared to leave Paris, the Arab men went into the bathroom, pulled the plumbing fixtures off the walls, and packed them with their luggage. They assumed that the power was in the fixtures themselves. They had no idea of the system of pipes that brought the water up to the spigot, and they actually believed they could install those fixtures inside their desert tents and have running water anytime they wished!

When Lawrence saw what the Arab men had done, he explained to them that the faucets were useless unless they were connected to pipes that were connected to a source of water. The Arabs' mistake seems foolish—until we realize that we fall prey to the same folly.

Paul's message in Galatians 3 is, don't try to get water from a disconnected fixture. Don't try to obtain spiritual power from a fixture that is not connected to Jesus the Son. Life and power come by grace through faith in the Lord Jesus. We cannot obtain life and power from the law or from doing good works or from church membership or from symbolic rituals.

The law is good, but it cannot save you. It's important to be involved in a local church, but church membership cannot save you. Outward symbols such as baptism and communion are a meaningful part of the Christian experience, but these symbols cannot save you.

Only Jesus saves. You must be connected to him. You must have a pipeline to God's grace, and that pipeline is faith in Jesus the Son.

But wait a minute—doesn't Paul say, "For as many of you as were baptized into Christ have put on Christ" (3:27). Isn't he saying that baptism saves us, and that we "put on Christ" through baptism? No, Paul is using "baptized into" to mean "identified with." When we accepted Christ as Lord and Savior, we became identified with Christ, we "put on Christ," we became clothed in Christ. Just as Jesus is the Son of the King, we also became children of the King.

The law of God no longer imprisons us, condemns us, and drives us to Christ in guilt and shame. Now the grace of God covers us, and the promise of God lifts us up. The promise God gave to Abraham is now our promise, and it breaks down all walls, all divisions, and binds us together in unity. As Paul writes: "There is neither Jew nor Greek, there is neither slave nor free, there is no male and female, for you are all one in Christ Jesus. And if you are Christ's, then you are Abraham's offspring, heirs according to promise" (3:28-29).

Our testimony to the fallen world is not, "See how good we are! See how perfectly we keep the law." Rather, our testimony is, "We are all sinners, and no one can keep the law. We were once broken and separated from God as you are, but God has given us the promise of his grace. He has clothed us in his power and righteousness and grace."

And that is good news—the best news this dying world has ever heard.

6

Until Christ Is Formed in You

Galatians 4

Why are so many Christians today anemic, ineffectual, defeated, and immature? Why do so many Christians start off on the straight path of godliness only to end up in a ditch, sidelined by immorality or defection from Christ? What is this disease that stunts the growth of so many believers today?

Paul, in Galatians 4, has the answer: *Christ is not formed in them.*

You may ask, "What does that mean? I don't think I've ever heard that phrase before. What does it mean to have Christ formed in me?"

This concept is rarely preached on or written about in the Christian community, yet I believe it is the key concept in Galatians 4. Paul writes, "my little children, for whom I am again in the anguish of childbirth until Christ is formed in you!" (4:19).

How do we know if people who claim to be Christians are genuine or not? We tend to draw conclusions from their actions. If they attend church, use the right evangelical vocabulary, put on a plastic

Christian smile (or, in some churches, a pious and vinegary frown), practice all the proper rituals, and express all the proper evangelical opinions—then we conclude they are genuine Christians. But none of these outward signs is proof that Christ is being formed in them.

A new Christian is like an empty glove. A glove without a hand in it is flat, limp, and useless. It can't do anything. It can't grasp anything, it can't flex its fingers, it can't move, it has no life or dynamism of its own.

But when I put my hand in that glove, it conforms to the shape and movement of my hand. My fingers and thumb can cause the glove to come alive with motion and strength. Everything my hand does the glove can do. My hand has been formed within that glove, and the glove takes on the form of my hand.

Can other people see my hand? No. It's hidden within the glove. But my hand is obviously the source of the power, life, and dynamism of the glove. No one looks at the glove and thinks, *What a strong, energetic, and skillful glove that is!* It's obvious to all that the power is not in the glove, but in the hand.

In a similar way, we are the glove, Christ is the hand. We are flat, limp, and useless until Christ is formed in us. We can't do anything in our own strength. We have no life or dynamism of our own. We become useful to God only when Christ is formed in us and when we become conformed to him. When we take on the shape and form and power of Jesus Christ, we become God's hands, and he can use us to accomplish his purpose in the world.

And that is why Paul says, "I am again in the anguish of childbirth until Christ is formed in you!"

No longer a slave but a son

As we come to Galatians 4, Paul has finished his theological argument and his doctrinal debate. He has already made his case for truth, and he is exhausted from the effort of exposing the deception of the Judaizers. Up to this point, Paul has appealed to the reason and intellect of the Galatian believers on the basis of doctrine and Scripture.

Now, Paul changes tack. He moves from rational argument to emotional appeal. He reminds the Galatian believers of the special relationship—the spiritual relationship—he has had with them. He reminds them of their initial response to the gospel.

There are three divisions in Galatians 4. In the first division, verses 1-11, Paul tells us that we are sons and daughters of the Living God. In the second division, verses 12-20, Paul tells us that the proof of our adoption as God's sons and daughters will be that Christ—God's only begotten Son and our older Brother—is formed in us. In the third division, verses 21-31, Paul tells us that we are children born of the Spirit, not of the flesh. Let's look at the first division of Galatians 4:

> I mean that the heir, as long as he is a child, is no different from a slave, though he is the owner of everything, but he is under guardians and managers until the date set by his father. In the same way we also, when we were children, were enslaved to the elementary principles of the world. But when the fullness of time had come, God sent forth his Son, born of woman, born under the law, to redeem those who were under the law, so that we might receive adoption as sons. And because you are sons, God has sent the Spirit of his Son into our hearts, crying, "Abba! Father!" So you are no longer a slave, but a son, and if a son, then an heir through God.
>
> Formerly, when you did not know God, you were enslaved to those that by nature are not gods. But now that you have come to know God, or rather to be known by God, how can you turn back again to the weak and

> worthless elementary principles of the world, whose slaves you want to be once more? You observe days and months and seasons and years! I am afraid I may have labored over you in vain (4:1-11).

Paul reminds the misguided Christians in Galatia that because the Son of God has come into the world, they have been transformed from slaves to full adopted sons, with every right to call God, "Abba! Father!"

The church of Galatia was a multicultural church. It embraced the Jewish culture, the Greek culture, and the Roman culture. All of the cultures of that region practiced an official ceremony when children reached adulthood.

In the Jewish culture, at age twelve, a boy who has been under his father's authority and control becomes responsible for himself. This transition takes place on the first Sabbath after the boy's *bar mitzvah* (which means "son of the commandment" or "son of the law"). At the ceremony, the father prays, "Blessed be thou, O God, who has taken from me the responsibility of this boy."

Then the boy would pray, "O my God, and God of my fathers, on this solemn and sacred day which marks my passage from boyhood to manhood, I humbly raise my eyes unto thee and declare with sincerity and truth that, henceforth, I will keep thy commandments and undertake to bear the responsibility of my actions toward thee."

With maturity comes personal responsibility.

In the Greek culture, boys came of age at eighteen. At this stage of life, the boy was called an *ephebe* or *ephebos*. He was inducted into the militia, and the community would take the boy, cut off his long hair, and offer the hair as a sacrifice to the god Apollo.

In the Roman culture, by the age of eighteen, a boy would exchange a child's robe (toga) for the robe of an adult. The family would hold a *liberalia* ceremony, celebrating the youth's liberation from childhood to adulthood. He would take his childhood toys and destroy them, offering them as a sacrifice to the gods as a sign that he was putting childhood behind him. This custom perhaps inspired Paul's words to the Corinthians: "When I was a child, I spoke like a child, I thought like a child, I reasoned like a child. When I became a man, I gave up childish ways" (1 Corinthians 13:11).

Paul uses this analogy to make a point: When Christ came into the world, the law's purpose was fulfilled. Christ ushered in the Age of Redemption. The law serves as a mirror to show men and women how sinful they are, in order to drive them to the grace of God through our Lord Jesus Christ.

When the Son of God was born into the world, he was born of a virgin, born of a woman, and thus both fully God and fully human. Though he was born in human flesh, he was kept sinless and perfect. Though he was born under the law, he kept it perfectly. Though he was coexistent with God the Father before time and space even existed, he learned obedience. As Hebrews 5:8 tells us, "Although he was a son, he learned obedience through what he suffered."

When the Son of God came into the world, he inherited all of his Father's estate, because he pleased the Father. When he came into the world, he was able to cry to God by the most endearing familial term, "Abba! Father!"

Paul pours his heart out

Someone once said to me, "I have been trying so hard to be a good person."

"You're doomed to fail," I replied. "You'll fail and fail until you get exhausted and depressed from trying and failing."

Paul is telling us that the Christian life is not a matter of trying hard, of gritting our teeth and giving holiness our best try. That's the path of legalism, and it's a dead-end street.

The Christian life is a matter of accepting the grace of God, receiving the call of Jesus, our Brother, signing our adoption papers, and receiving the gift of inheritance with all its responsibilities and privileges. Because we are sons, God has sent the Spirit of his Son, Jesus, into our hearts, so that we, too, can cry to God, "Abba! Father!" We are no longer slaves but children and heirs of God.

Like the Christians in Galatia, we are tempted to forget our royal adoption, and we settle for living like paupers. We are tempted to forget our princely position, and we behave like beggars. We are tempted to forget our priestly calling, and we rely on legalistic performance.

I can imagine that Paul had tears streaming down his cheeks as he wrote in verse 11, "I am afraid I may have labored over you in vain." It's as if he were saying to them, "All the miles I've traveled, all the illnesses I've suffered, all the loneliness I've endured, all the imprisonment and punishment I have survived—was it all for nothing? If you go back into legalism, into slavery, into pleasing people instead of pleasing God, then everything I did to bring you to Christ was wasted effort."

Proof of adoption

Beginning with verse 12, Paul pleads with the believers in Galatia, reminding them in strong, emotional terms of all they meant to him, and all he meant to them:

> Brothers, I entreat you, become as I am, for I also have become as you are. You did me no wrong. You know it was because of a bodily ailment that I preached the gospel to you at first, and though my condition was a trial to you, you did not scorn or despise me, but received me as an angel of God, as Christ Jesus. What then has become of your blessedness? For I testify to you that, if possible, you

would have gouged out your eyes and given them to me.
Have I then become your enemy by telling you the truth?
They make much of you, but for no good purpose. They
want to shut you out, that you may make much of them.
It is always good to be made much of for a good purpose,
and not only when I am present with you (4:12-18).

Paul had enjoyed an extremely close relationship with the Galatian Christians, but now the relationship was breached. There was
a chill between the apostle and these saints. The Judaizers had not
only undermined Paul's reputation and the beliefs of the Galatian
Christians, but they had also undermined the deep friendship Paul
had enjoyed with these churches.

Here, after strongly, logically refuting the error of the Judaizers,
Paul takes a moment to focus on his personal relationship with the
Christians in Galatia. Paul was a master psychologist. He understood human nature—and he knew there was a strong likelihood
that these Christians, on reading the blunt and critical portions of
the letter, might become defensive.

When people become defensive, they often cannot hear what
you are saying to them. They become focused on defending their
own position. So Paul wisely devoted a section of this letter to an
emotional appeal to the Galatian Christians. He urged them to
remember the Christian love and friendship they had shared, and
all the kindness they had shown him in the past. The last thing
Paul wanted was to deepen the division between himself and these
believers.

Whenever the truth of God is compromised, that compromise
brings division. Broken relationships are almost always a conse-
quence of sin and error. Here in Galatians 4, Paul tries to heal the
broken relationship by reminding the Galatians of their close relationship in the past and expressing his tender feelings for them in

the present. That's why, in verse 19, he refers to them as "my little children"—an expression used frequently by John, "the apostle of love," but rarely by Paul. Clearly, Paul wants them to be assured of his love, a deep and parental kind of love.

So Paul pours his heart out to the Galatians. He tells them, in effect, "I love you. I care about you more than I can say. The reason I say these things is that I care deeply about your spiritual well-being."

Paul begins by saying, "Brothers, I entreat you…" In other words, "Brothers, I beg you, I plead with you!" We can preach and cajole and try every method in the book to reach people for Christ, but if they do not sense our compassion and genuine love for them, if they don't hear in our voices that we desperately want them to escape hell and judgment, then all our words will fall on deaf ears. It will be just another opinion, just one more philosophy out of the many competing philosophies in this world.

Whenever you and I need to confront others about sin or error in their lives, it's important that we focus not only on the issue but also on the relationship. It's important that we speak the language of love, not just the language of truth. Our goal should never be merely to set people straight, but to bring healing, restoration, and an even stronger relationship in the Lord.

In verses 13-14, Paul says it was because of a physical illness that he first preached to the Galatian Christians. He had apparently suffered from a debilitating illness that forced him to stay in Galatia for some time. While he was there, he preached the gospel and founded these churches. We don't know what illness Paul suffered from— he doesn't tell us, and Bible scholars have speculated on that question for centuries. But Paul makes it clear that the illness made him repulsive and caused him to be a burden on the Galatians.

Yet the Galatian believers received him, cared for him, and loved him in spite of his pathetic condition. Far from being revolted by his illness, they counted it a privilege to serve him and care for his physical needs. They received him as if he were an angel of God, as if he were Christ himself.

Why did they receive him so warmly? There can be only one answer: The message of salvation that Paul brought them was so beautiful that it canceled out the ugliness of Paul's physical malady. As the prophet Isaiah wrote:

> How beautiful upon the mountains
>> are the feet of him who brings good news,
> who publishes peace, who brings good news of
>> happiness,
>> who publishes salvation,
>> who says to Zion, "Your God reigns."
>>> (Isaiah 52:7)

The Galatian Christians responded not to the apostle's appalling appearance but to his beautiful message. He brought good news of peace, joy, and salvation. So, regardless of his affliction, regardless of his appearance, they had received Paul as if he were the most handsome man alive.

Why was there now a chill in their relationship? Because of the lies of the Judaizers. These legalists had slandered the good news of salvation that Paul originally brought to Galatia, and they had slandered Paul himself. They had driven a wedge between Paul and the Galatian believers. So Paul asks, "Have I then become your enemy by telling you the truth?"

I can tell you from personal experience that nothing tears out the heart of a pastor, Bible teacher, or youth minister like seeing someone they have led to the Lord turn away from the faith. The defection of the Galatians tore the heart of Paul. We can only imagine how such spiritual defection wounds the heart of God.

Many Christian converts appreciate a preacher or teacher as long as he says what they want to hear. But the moment he confronts them with a hard truth (such as, "it's not God's will for you to marry an unbeliever," or "a premarital sexual relationship goes against God's Word," or "that popular teacher is spreading false doctrines"), those converts often turn against him and seek out another preacher who will say what they want to hear. I've seen it happen many times.

Paul was quick to point out that his feelings for the Galatian believers had not changed. He still viewed them with a tender and parental love. He still viewed them as his own children in the faith. He still remembered their warmth and affection for him. They would have gouged out their own eyes and given them to him if it would have eased his affliction. (The eye-gouging image is a Middle Eastern expression of intense affection, like saying, "I would die for you.")

Paul goes on to explain the motivation of the Judaizers: "They make much of you, but for no good purpose" (4:17). In other words, the Judaizers sidle up to you and flatter you and want to be your friends—but they are up to no good. Paul adds, "They want to shut you out, that you may make much of them." In other words, the Judaizers want to pull you into their orbit and shut you out of Paul's life and Paul's gospel message, so that you can become *their* disciples, enslaved by their false gospel.

Jesus pointed out this same scheming spirit in the scribes and Pharisees: "Woe to you, scribes and Pharisees, hypocrites! For you travel across sea and land to make a single proselyte, and when he becomes a proselyte, you make him twice as much a child of hell as yourselves" (Matthew 23:15). The flattery of these Judaizers probably was one of the principal reasons the Galatians were so easily "bewitched." Paul warns them not to fall for the flattery, because it is all self-serving and deceptive, intended to lead the Galatians into deadly error.

In various forms, these Judaizers are still with us today. Many people use religion as a way of building up their own power, expanding their personal influence, making disciples for themselves, becoming "church bosses" disguised as Christian leaders. They use flattery and charm to worm their way into the church and to catch believers off guard. In the end, they create destruction and division and lead well-intentioned people into error and sin.

Paul did not want the Galatian believers to be followers of Paul. He wanted them to be followers of the Lord Jesus Christ. And above all, he wanted them to become Christlike and to have Christ formed in them.

A radical change within

We now come to the key verse of Galatians 4. Here, Paul tells the Galatian believers that outward maturity and outward appearances don't impress God. It's what's inside that counts:

> ...my little children, for whom I am again in the anguish of childbirth until Christ is formed in you! (4:19)

The affection Paul bears toward them is not merely a parental affection but specifically a *motherly* affection. "My little children," he says, "for whom I am again in the anguish of childbirth." The first time he felt this anguish was when he initially preached the gospel to them and led them to the Lord. Now he is again in anguish because they have been lured away from the gospel, and he must lead them back to the grace of God once again.

Paul was there in the delivery room for their spiritual birth. He nursed them on the pure milk of the Word of God. But now they are behaving as if they need to be spiritually born all over again. He is saying, in effect, "You make me feel like a mother who has to deliver the same baby twice!"

The apostle Paul wants to see a visible and outward sign of a radical change within them. He wants to see the shape of the hand filling the glove. He wants to see Christ formed within these Galatian believers.

He is telling them, "Christ will not be formed in you by your list of dos and don'ts. He will not be formed in you by all the rules you keep and the rituals you perform. He will not be formed in you while you ignore his will for your life. He will not be formed in you while you neglect his Word. He will not be formed in you while you spend money on material things and pleasures and status symbols instead of giving generously to advance the kingdom of God."

Do you truly want Christ to be formed in you? Will you make yourself available so that he can be formed in you? Do you want him to fill every corner of your life? Do you want Christ to live and move freely in your life, as the hand lives and moves freely in the glove?

I can tell you, based on the authority of the Word of God, that the Lord Jesus Christ wants to replace your weakness with his strength, your folly with his wisdom, your greed with his grace, your lust with his love, your problems with his peace, your jealousy with his joy, your cowardice with his courage. I can tell you, on the authority of Scripture, that God does not care about your Dun and Bradstreet rating or your credit score. He is not concerned with your social standing or the square footage of your house or the kind of car you drive. He wants to know if you are available. He wants to know if you are going to give him the entire glove of your life or if you are going to withhold a few fingers—because he can't do anything with half a glove.

In order for Christ to be formed in you, you must be fully available, fully surrendered, nothing withheld, nothing hidden from God. The proof that our faith is real, and that we have been adopted by God, is that Christ is being formed in us. Without the evidence that he lives in us and animates our being and carries out his will through our lives, there is no outward sign that we genuinely belong to him.

Children of the promise

Finally, the apostle Paul reminds the Galatian believers that they are children of a spiritual covenant:

> I wish I could be present with you now and change my tone, for I am perplexed about you.
>
> Tell me, you who desire to be under the law, do you not listen to the law? For it is written that Abraham had two sons, one by a slave woman and one by a free woman. But the son of the slave was born according to the flesh, while the son of the free woman was born through promise. Now this may be interpreted allegorically: these women are two covenants. One is from Mount Sinai, bearing children for slavery; she is Hagar. Now Hagar is Mount Sinai in Arabia; she corresponds to the present Jerusalem, for she is in slavery with her children. But the Jerusalem above is free, and she is our mother. For it is written,
>
> > "Rejoice, O barren one who does not bear;
> >   break forth and cry aloud, you who are not in labor!
> > For the children of the desolate one will be more
> >   than those of the one who has a husband."
>
> Now you, brothers, like Isaac, are children of promise. But just as at that time he who was born according to the flesh persecuted him who was born according to the Spirit, so also it is now. But what does the Scripture say? "Cast out the slave woman and her son, for the son of the slave woman shall not inherit with the son of the free woman." So, brothers, we are not children of the slave but of the free woman (4:20-31).

Here Paul draws a contrast between two sons, Isaac and Ishmael, and between two mothers, Sarah and Hagar. Sarah and her son Isaac were Abraham's wife and son according to God's perfect will and according to God's promise. Ishmael and Hagar, by contrast, were a result of Sarah and Abraham trying to improvise and help God out. Whenever we try to improve on God's plan, whenever we try to get ahead of the Lord, whenever we try to hurry God's promises along—*we bring about disaster!*

In the case of Isaac and Ishmael, the disaster Abraham and Sarah caused has lasted four thousand years. The descendants of Isaac are the Jews. The descendants of Ishmael are the Arabs. The enmity between the descendants of Isaac and the descendants of Ishmael continues to this day. The attention of the world is constantly focused on the clash between Isaac's descendants and Ishmael's descendants. Their strife makes headlines on a near-daily basis.

What does Paul's Isaac and Ishmael analogy mean for your life and mine? Paul is telling us that we are heirs and children of the promise God made to Abraham. We are the children of grace. We are the children of mercy and forgiveness.

Like Isaac, we have been spiritually conceived and spiritually adopted by God the Father for the sake of our older Brother, Jesus. We must not go back to the law. We must not go back into slavery to legalism, becoming children of the slave woman instead of the free woman.

Why live as a child of slavery when we can enjoy the freedom of God's grace and forgiveness? Why live as a child of outcasts when we can enjoy the blessings of being God's adopted heirs? Why try to improvise and improve on God's will when he already has a glorious future planned for us? Why live as rejected children when our Abba, our Daddy, our heavenly Father loves us?

So what are the practical steps to becoming children of the

promise, children of grace? What are the practical steps to having Christ formed in us?

There are none!

That is the whole point Paul has been making. Becoming children of the promise and having Christ formed in us is not a matter of something we do or steps we take. If having Christ formed in us depends on our actions, our work, our willpower, our obedience to certain rules and rituals, then we are right back in the legalism trap. We are back in slavery.

All we have to do to become children of the promise, children of grace, is to surrender to the Lord Jesus Christ. It's a matter of saying to Jesus, "I'm setting aside my agenda, my will, my wants, and I am laying them all at your feet. I'm holding nothing back. I'm hiding nothing from you. Let me be nothing more than a glove on your hand. Do whatever you want with me, to me, and through me."

That's not a prayer we can pray once and for all. We need to pray that prayer again and again, every day, every hour, and whenever we are tempted to take back control of our lives. We will fail, we will falter, and we will have to continually return to him and renew that commitment.

But if we live our lives with the goal of allowing Christ to be formed in us, then gradually, over time, we will see *our* character, *our* will, and *our* desires become increasingly like his. We will hear ourselves say, "Not my will, but yours be done."

Not only will we see change in our lives and in our desires, but the people around us will see a change in us as well. They will see our lives begin to look more and more like the life Jesus lived. People will hear us saying the things Jesus said. They will see us doing the things Jesus did. The good news of Jesus Christ will pour forth from our lives, and people will be blessed and drawn to him.

All of these wonderful things will happen *not* because we tried harder to keep God's law or obey Jesus' teachings or practice religious rites and rituals. They will happen because we stopped trying, and simply let Jesus take over and live his life through us. They will happen because we allowed Christ to be formed in us, so that our flat and shapeless lives could take on the form and shape of his life.

If you have read *The Voyage of the Dawn Treader* by C.S. Lewis, you undoubtedly remember Eustace Scrubb, the sullen, obnoxious, and self-centered cousin of the Pevensie children. The book begins with the memorable line, "There was a boy called Eustace Clarence Scrubb, and he almost deserved it." Eustace, along with Lucy and Edmund Pevensie, is drawn into an adventure in Narnia aboard a ship called the *Dawn Treader*.

Throughout the early part of the voyage, Eustace continually complains and makes a nuisance of himself. At one point, the *Dawn Treader* drops anchor at an unexplored island. Eustace goes ashore, wanders off, and stumbles onto a dragon's treasure hoard. He greedily revels in all the wealth he has discovered, and he places a golden bracelet on his arm. Then, thinking "greedy, dragonish thoughts" as he becomes drowsy, he falls asleep on top of the dragon's treasure.

When Eustace awakens, he discovers that he is no longer a boy but a dragon. He has been transformed while he slept. The bracelet, which fit comfortably on his arm when he was a boy, is now painfully small for his dragon leg. He is forced to remain in that state for six days. Then he encounters a majestic lion—who, of course, is Aslan, who symbolizes the Lord Jesus Christ in Lewis's Narnia tales.

Aslan takes dragon-Eustace to a garden with a healing pool of water and tells him that he may go into the water after he undresses. Eustace is confused because, being a dragon, he has no clothes to shed. But then he realizes that, being a dragon, he can shed his skin like a snake. He scratches at his scaly dragon's skin, and every time he sheds one skin, he finds another underneath. Then another and another. In despair, Eustace finally understands he is incapable of removing his skin.

Then Aslan says, "You will have to let me undress you." Eustace is afraid to allow Aslan's claws to come near him. He is afraid to open himself up to Aslan's will for his life. He is afraid to surrender. Yet, because of the pain of the bracelet and the pain of being a dragon, Eustace's desperation overcomes his fear. He submits to the lion, and Aslan goes to work.

Aslan tears and rips at the dragon with his claws, and the ripping and rending are so deep and painful that Eustace thinks Aslan is killing him! Finally, all the dragon flesh has been torn away, and Aslan throws Eustace into the healing water. When Eustace emerges, he comes out clean and human. Aslan then dresses Eustace in new clothes, and from then on, Eustace is a changed lad, no longer obnoxious and self-centered, but helpful, courteous, and courageous.

It is Lewis's parable of what it means to have Christ formed in us. You and I are no different from Eustace Scrubb. We cannot "undragon" ourselves by our own efforts. But if we surrender to the Lord Jesus, if we allow him to perform his healing work in our lives, we will experience the miracle of transformation when Christ is formed in us.

7

Liberated in Christ

Galatians 5:1-14

In recent years, we have seen many theological movements sweep through the church and the culture—liberation theology, black liberation theology, feminist theology, restoration theology, the emerging church, and on and on. For some theologians and seminary professors, the plain truth of God's Word is not enough. They have to come up with some new creative twist to make the Christian faith more "relevant" to our times. The problem is, these creative reinterpretations of Scripture always end up substituting worldly philosophy in place of God's truth.

One of these movements that has invaded many churches is called "struggle theology." According to struggle theology, we are all sinners—so far, so good, the Bible agrees with that. But struggle theology goes on to say that no one can ever have victory over sin. God's promise that "all things are possible" (Matthew 19:26) is not to be taken literally. There are no simple answers, no easy solutions, no absolutes, and no victories—only struggles. Don't set yourself up for disappointment by choosing a role model of perfection like Jesus Christ; instead, choose a role model who claims to be a Christian, but who fails and sins regularly. This will help you to feel better about yourself when you fail and sin. What they actually mean is that your continuous habitual and deliberate sin does not matter.

Whereas the Bible defines *sin* as violating God's will, falling short of God's perfection, and breaking the relationship between us and God, struggle theology redefines sin as an emotional affliction caused by poor self-esteem, childhood issues, environmental influence, and even genetic deficiencies. The Bible says that when Christ is formed in you, you *hate* sin; struggle theology tells us we must *understand* sin. The Bible says that the cure for sin is salvation through faith in Jesus Christ; struggle theology says that the best news we can hope for (and it's not really very good news at all) is that everybody struggles with sin, and that's okay.

According to struggle theology, God is merciful—again, so far, so good, the Bible agrees with that too. But then struggle theologians go too far, saying that God is nonjudgmental, he is understanding of our choosing to sin, he is accommodating toward our acceptance of sin, and he's really okay with our not feeling remorse when we sin, as long as we are struggling with it. The struggle theologians tell us that God understands our need for lust and adultery. He understands that we need to lie to our spouse and cheat on our taxes. He understands our need to cook the books and fib on our expense accounts at work. And if you have to abandon your family for the sake of a new romance, or to pursue your personal success, well, he understands that too. As long as you're struggling, God is okay with that.

The advocates of struggle theology think they have come up with something new, a novel twist on the old-time religion. But there is nothing new about struggle theology. This is the oldest delusion in the Book.

The first struggle theologian in history was Eve, the wife of Adam. When Satan came to her and tempted her to eat the forbidden fruit, she didn't take him up on it right away. Eve dialogued with Satan, and Satan questioned Eve. She could have said, "Thus says the Lord, end of story, and now beat it, you snake in the grass!" But she didn't. Instead, she struggled with temptation. She struggled with Satan. And the end result of struggle theology is always giving in to sin.

The struggle is all about putting on appearances. The struggle is the self-deluding act we put on as we rationalize yielding to sin (and we knew all along we were planning to give in). The struggle is about convincing ourselves that, even though we ultimately give in to sin, we are really good people. We never really planned to sin—we had good intentions, we struggled, but we lost. Oh well.

Our declaration of freedom in Christ

God never intended that the Christian life should be a continuous losing struggle against sin. God wants us to have complete victory over sin. Jesus lived and died and rose again to give us that victory. When God, in his Word, promises us triumph and deliverance from sin, when he tells us we are more than conquerors and that all things are possible to those who believe, this is not mere hyperbole. This is God's unalterable truth.

It's ironic that in this age—an age when so many people revel in their so-called freedom to flout the laws of man and God, to treat each other with contempt, to run roughshod over anyone who gets in the way of their selfish ambition, to gratify the senses with drugs, alcohol, pornography, and promiscuous sex—people live in absolute slavery. They are slaves to drugs, alcohol, tobacco, cocaine, gambling, and their own appetites and lusts. The more people assert their self-centered freedom, the more they become enslaved by sin.

The Lord Jesus Christ offers his followers freedom from addiction.

To those who repent, he offers liberation from sin and destructive habits. The key theme of Galatians 5 is *liberty!* Here Paul tells us about true liberation, authentic freedom. Here he reveals the secret of victory and triumph in the life of the believer. Christian freedom is the very heart of the gospel of Jesus Christ. Freedom is the essence of godly living.

This is not some new doctrine that the apostle Paul invented. Freedom was the heart of the message that Jesus himself preached during his earthly ministry. He said, "If you abide in my word, you are truly my disciples, and you will know the truth, and the truth will set you free...Truly, truly, I say to you, everyone who practices sin is a slave to sin. The slave does not remain in the house forever; the son remains forever. So if the Son sets you free, you will be free indeed" (John 8:31-32,34-36). Paul opens Galatians 5 by echoing the message of the Lord Jesus:

> For freedom Christ has set us free; stand firm therefore, and do not submit again to a yoke of slavery (5:1).

Here is the Christian's declaration of freedom in Christ. What was the basic doctrinal error of the Judaizers? It's the same error committed by every religious system that relies on human ingenuity. The Judaizers prided themselves on their works, on keeping the law. Specifically, they prided themselves on circumcision.

Instead of seeing circumcision as an outward symbol of God's gracious promise to Abraham, they saw circumcision as having spiritual value. Instead of treating circumcision as a symbol of God's desire to purify the human heart from sin, the Judaizers saw it as the means of salvation. Instead of seeing circumcision as an outward sign of God's covenant, they saw it as the covenant itself.

Make no mistake: Christian freedom is a dangerous idea. Paul knew that. Whenever you give people freedom, there's always a risk they will abuse that freedom. In fact, that was one of the Judaizers' arguments against Christian freedom. They claimed that if people were no longer required to keep the law in order to be saved, they would think they had a license to sin and would become a lawless and rebellious people.

But Paul rejects this claim. His arguments about Christian freedom proceed logically from his statement in Galatians 4:19—"my little children, for whom I am again in the anguish of childbirth until Christ is formed in you!" The Christian who has Christ formed in him or her is not going to become lawless and rebellious. The Christian who is sealed by the Spirit of God, who does not deliberately grieve the Spirit but seeks to please God, will not live in rebellion against the standards of God.

The ironic truth is that the legalist is the one who must ultimately rebel against God because the legalist is living in bondage. He's a slave, depending entirely on rituals and outward observance, depending on his own efforts, depending on his "struggle" to remain true to God. It is the nature of a slave to rebel against his master.

So, while Christian freedom is a dangerous idea, legalism is infinitely more dangerous because legalism attempts to do the impossible. Legalism is an attempt to restrain and confine and control the behavior of human beings whose hearts have never been changed. It can't be done. Legalism can never succeed. The human heart can never be controlled by the law; it must be transformed by grace.

Trading God's riches for spiritual poverty

Paul goes on to make a devastating argument, proving that legalism and the grace of Jesus Christ cannot coexist:

> Look: I, Paul, say to you that if you accept circumcision, Christ will be of no advantage to you. I testify again to every man who accepts circumcision that he is obligated

to keep the whole law. You are severed from Christ, you who would be justified by the law; you have fallen away from grace. For through the Spirit, by faith, we ourselves eagerly wait for the hope of righteousness. For in Christ Jesus neither circumcision nor uncircumcision counts for anything, but only faith working through love (5:2-6).

Paul says, in effect, "If you think you can overcome sin by your own struggle, then why believe in Christ? What good does it do to say you follow Christ if you are still going to be a slave to the law? If you are still a slave to the law, then Christ is of no value to you. If you think circumcision saves you, then you have an obligation to keep the entire law, perfectly and flawlessly. But in Christ, it doesn't matter if you are circumcised or not. The only thing that matters is that you have placed your faith and trust in him."

The person who struggles to earn his salvation by keeping the law is in a zero-tolerance situation. One sin and you're done. Break one tiny provision of the law one time, and you might as well have broken the entire law a hundred times a day.

Suppose you are driving down the street and you are inattentive for just one moment—and you drive right through an intersection without stopping at the stop sign. A policeman on a motorcycle sees you and pulls you over. What is your defense?

"But officer," you might say, "I don't steal. I don't commit adultery. I've never killed anyone! I have always been a law-abiding citizen, and I have never broken any other law."

Will the police officer be impressed? Will he pin a medal on you as a reward for all the laws you did *not* break? No. He's going to write you a ticket for breaking the law, for failing to stop at a stop sign.

All your other good works are commendable, but you still broke the law. The police officer doesn't care how many laws you kept. He saw you break the law, and you are going to have to pay the penalty.

The law cannot save you because you cannot keep the entire law. You will inevitably break the law, no matter how hard you try to keep it, no matter how hard you struggle not to sin. If you think you can keep the law perfectly and earn your own salvation, then you are deceived, just as the Galatians were deceived by the Judaizers.

What sets us free? We can be set free only by the righteousness of Christ, the power of Christ, and the justification that is in Christ. Nothing else in the universe can liberate us from the enslaving power of sin.

In verse 4, Paul says, "You are severed from Christ, you who would be justified by the law; you have fallen away from grace." Is Paul saying that the Galatian believers have lost their salvation? Absolutely not. Nine times in this epistle Paul refers to the Galatians as "brothers." He's addressing the Judaizers, and he's sounding a warning to any Galatians who are on the verge of being persuaded by the Judaizers.

He is making a statement of simple logic: If you think you are justified by keeping the law, you have fallen away from grace, you have rejected God's grace. If you put your trust in rituals, ceremonies, traditions, and other trappings of legalism, you have left no room in your life for grace.

You either put your trust in the law or in grace. You can't be saved by both law and grace, because they are mutually exclusive. When a follower of Christ tries to live a life of struggle instead of accepting the freedom of God's grace, he has exchanged grace for slavery to the law. He has exchanged freedom for bondage.

Those who enjoy the liberty of God's grace will live in a way that is obedient to God's law—but their motive will be completely opposite that of the legalist. The legalist tries to obey the law out of fear; the believer obeys out of gratitude to God. The legalist tries to earn salvation; the believer obeys because he's already saved by grace through faith. The legalist never knows if he has done enough; the believer trusts in the all-sufficient sacrifice of the Lord Jesus.

The legalist cannot enjoy the richness of God's grace. He has exchanged God's riches for a life of spiritual poverty, toil, and suffering. He has exchanged victory in Christ for a life of defeat, fear, and guilt. He has exchanged a life of heavenly luxury for the spiritual equivalent of living under a bridge. He has fallen away from grace and tumbled into poverty, struggle, and legalistic futility.

I once heard of a young man who scrimped and saved his money to book passage on a ship to Europe. During his journey, whenever the mealtime announcement came over the public address system, this young man would rush to his cabin. His fellow passengers wondered why he disappeared at every mealtime. The food on the voyage was sumptuous, yet this young man never joined them at the table. He would hide in his cabin instead.

Finally, near the end of the journey, some of the people who had befriended him on the voyage asked, "Why don't you eat with us?"

With shame and embarrassment, the young man confessed, "I scraped together every dollar I could just to buy a ticket for the voyage. I can't afford to buy a meal aboard ship. So I go to my cabin and eat cheese and crackers that I brought on board."

His fellow voyagers were astounded. "Didn't you know?" they asked him. "Didn't anyone tell you that your ticket included all meals? You've been subsisting on cheese and crackers when you could have been feasting on all that sumptuous food!"

If you are a believer in the Lord Jesus Christ and you are living a life of legalism, a life of struggle, then you need to take a clear-eyed, objective look at your life. Ask yourself, *Am I subsisting on the spiritual equivalent of cheese and crackers when I could be feasting on the grace of the Lord Jesus Christ? Am I hiding out in a tiny little cabin of legalism when I could be enjoying the abundant life in Christ?*

We have all sinned, and there is a price to be paid for sin—but the price is not legalism. The price is far beyond what you and I could ever afford. That's the bad news. But here's the good news: Jesus already paid the price so you and I don't have to. That's grace! He paid not only for our eternal salvation, but he paid for us to experience freedom and the abundant life throughout our journey to heaven.

Whenever you find yourself feeling anxious and fearful that you are not observing all sorts of rituals, whenever you find yourself irritated because some little detail of the church service is not quite up to your exacting standards, whenever you find yourself asking, "Have I done enough to earn God's favor and approval?"…*stop*!

Remember Paul's warning that if you think you are justified by the law, "you have fallen away from grace." If you are trying to be saved by your own efforts and personal struggle, you are dishonoring the sacrifice of Christ and the abundant grace of God. If you are trying to earn God's approval, you need to be spiritually revived and restored. You need Spirit-to-spirit resuscitation from the Holy Spirit himself.

Two deadly streams

Next, Paul goes on to tell the Galatians—in surprisingly blunt terms—how destructive and damaging these deceivers, the Judaizers, are and what they deserve:

> You were running well. Who hindered you from obeying the truth? This persuasion is not from him who calls you. A little leaven leavens the whole lump. I have confidence in the Lord that you will take no other view, and the one who is troubling you will bear the penalty, whoever he is. But if I, brothers, still preach circumcision, why am I still being persecuted? In that case the offense of the

cross has been removed. I wish those who unsettle you would emasculate themselves! (5:7-12).

Paul lists five traits of these legalistic Judaizers:

1. They hinder obedience to God's truth.
2. They are not of God, who called the Galatian Christians.
3. Like yeast in a lump of dough, their false gospel contaminates the entire church.
4. They will be judged by God for their sin and deception.
5. They persecute those (like Paul) who preach the true gospel of God's grace.

Paul contrasts the Judaizers and their deception with the Galatian believers who came to Christ by believing the truth of the gospel:

> For you were called to freedom, brothers. Only do not use your freedom as an opportunity for the flesh, but through love serve one another (5:13).

Paul recognizes that there will be those in the church who will pervert his message of liberty in Christ, saying, "By God's grace, I'm free! I'm free to sin, I'm free to ignore God's moral demands, and I'm free to reject God's will for my life, because he will accept me by grace no matter what I do." Up to this point, Paul has been preaching against the extremism of legalism; but here in verse 13, he confronts the extremism of license.

The legalists thought they could please God by keeping a grocery list of dos and don'ts. Those on the other extreme—let's call them the "libertines"—prided themselves on rejecting all rules and moral codes. "I'm not bound by any laws like those poor, pathetic legalists," they would say. "I'm free to indulge all my lusts and desires. God's grace is my 'Get Out of Jail Free' card. I'm free to do anything I want, and Jesus will pick up the tab for all my sins."

You are undoubtedly familiar with the great words of "Amazing Grace" by John Newton. As the title proclaims, it is a song about God's grace. The second stanza reads:

> 'Twas grace that taught my heart to fear.
> And grace my fears relieved.
> How precious did that grace appear,
> The hour I first believed.

A church that caters to the "gay pride" community has rewritten the lyrics of that precious hymn. Not surprisingly, the rewriter appears to have no understanding of the biblical concept of grace. This writer eliminates all three appearances of the word *grace* from that stanza, replacing *grace* with *guilt* and *pride*:

> 'Twas guilt that taught my heart to fear.
> And pride my fears relieved;
> How precious did that pride appear,
> The hour I first believed!

John Newton, a repentant slave ship captain, had a clear, profound, and intense understanding of grace. He knew it was God's mercy and grace that brought fear into his life—because that fear drove John Newton to God. And he knew that it was grace, not pride, that drew him to a saving faith in Jesus Christ.

The libertine who takes pride in his sin is no closer to grace then the legalist who takes pride in his good works and rituals. To those who put their trust in the grace of God, there is no room for pride—neither legalistic pride nor libertine (licentious) pride. Both trample the grace of God underfoot.

The "believer" who chooses the libertine lifestyle of sinning freely and proudly, counting on God's grace to save him in spite of his lack of repentance, does not understand grace at all—and probably has not truly received grace. Those who have genuinely received Christ as Lord and Savior, who truly love Christ and cling to him in faith, would never trample on his sacrifice on the cross.

A genuine believer understands the lavish grace of God, and is so struck with gratitude and wonder that the very thought of sinning against God's grace is horrifying to him. His grasp of the true nature of grace helps deter him from sin. Yes, he will still sin—but he will never rationalize sinning by saying, "Oh, well, I'm covered by grace. I'm forgiven. Jesus died so I can sin all I want without any consequences."

Picture *legalism* and *libertinism* as two parallel streams of water that flow across our path, forming a barrier between earth and heaven. The stream of legalism flows with clear, sparkling water, the pure water of God's law—but because the demands of the law are so extreme and harsh, the stream flows furiously, and you cannot enter those waters without being drowned or smashed against the rocks.

The waters of the other stream, the stream of libertinism, flow calmly, quietly, placidly—and it seems its waters would be easy to cross. But the stream of libertinism is so contaminated with the pollution of sin that those waters would poison you and burn your flesh before you made it across.

Both the stream of legalism and the stream of libertinism are uncrossable and deadly. But there is still a way to travel safely from earth to heaven. Those two streams are spanned by the bridge of grace, the bridge of the gospel of Jesus Christ. By grace through faith, you can simply walk across without being smashed and battered by the waters of legalism, and without being poisoned and polluted by the waters of sin and libertinism.

The reason those two streams are deadly is that they are a man's way to God. Our Lord did not invent legalism and he did not invent libertinism. Those are purely human inventions.

The gospel of Jesus Christ leads to life because it is God's way to heaven. God gave the promise of grace to Abraham. God fulfilled the promise of grace through Jesus Christ. Grace is God's invention, and that is why grace leads to life.

Spiritual strongholds

Loving God and living in the richness of his grace will accomplish four important goals in your life. We see those four goals listed for us in these verses:

> For you were called to freedom, brothers. Only do not use your freedom as an opportunity for the flesh, but through love serve one another. For the whole law is fulfilled in one word: "You shall love your neighbor as yourself" (5:13-14).

What are the four goals we see in these verses?

The first goal: Living by God's grace prevents us from indulging the flesh and living to sin. Paul says we are not to use our freedom as an opportunity for the flesh.

The second goal: Living by God's grace motivates us to serve others. "Through love," Paul writes, "serve one another."

The third goal: Living by God's grace enables us to fulfill God's moral law. The great irony of legalism versus grace is that those who try to keep the law end up breaking it, yet those who live by God's grace and God's love end up fulfilling the entire law. For the whole law is fulfilled, Paul says, if we keep this one command: "You shall love your neighbor as yourself."

The fourth goal: Living by God's grace enables us to stop hating, hurting, and harming each other. As Christians, saved by grace through faith, we now live to love one another in the church, the body of Jesus Christ—and we live to show Christ's love to the world.

If you know Jesus as your Lord and Savior, if you know you are justified by grace yet you realize you have fallen into the deception of either legalism or libertinism, then there's a danger you should be aware of. There's a possibility that, by abandoning the liberty of God's grace, you may have allowed Satan and your own fallen flesh (your human sin nature) to establish a stronghold in your life—a stronghold you may be unable to break out of.

What is a stronghold? The word refers to a heavily defended fortress. The Old Testament contains many references to strongholds—fortresses with such strong walls and battlements that they are almost invulnerable to enemy attacks. In one of his letters to the church at Corinth, Paul writes of strongholds as satanic fortresses within the human soul and spirit—towering fortresses that our ancient enemy uses against us during a siege of spiritual warfare: "For the weapons of our warfare are not of the flesh but have divine power to destroy strongholds" (2 Corinthians 10:4).

This is a corollary to what Paul wrote about spiritual warfare in another letter: "For we do not wrestle against flesh and blood, but against the rulers, against the authorities, against the cosmic powers over this present darkness, against the spiritual forces of evil in the heavenly places" (Ephesians 6:12).

How do we know if there is a spiritual war taking place within us? How do we know if one of these spiritual strongholds exists within us? It might be a stronghold in your *thought patterns*:

- Patterns of defeatist thinking: "I never do anything right." "God can't use a loser like me." "God must not love me." "Why do I get all the bad luck?"
- Patterns of envy and jealousy: "Why does God give him success but not me?" "Why is she marrying Prince Charming while I'm still lonely?" "Why is everybody happy except me?"

- Patterns of fear and anxiety: "I can't trust God to protect me." "I can't trust God to do what's best for me." "What if God lets go of me?"
- Patterns of performance and people-pleasing: "What will people think of me if they find out I'm a Christian? Better keep my mouth shut!" "I'll go along with my friends tonight, and do the things they do. I don't want them to think I'm weird and religious."
- Patterns of lust and evil thoughts: "It doesn't hurt to look, does it?" "There's no harm in having these thoughts in my imagination as long as I don't act on them." "So what's the harm in a little Internet porn or Facebook flirting— as long as my spouse never catches me?"
- Patterns of deception and lying: "I can't let people know who I really am or what I really believe." "I can't take responsibility for this mistake. I might lose my job." "I can't tell my spouse the *real* reason I'm late tonight!"

The satanic stronghold that afflicts your soul might be exhibited in your *behavior patterns*:

- Addiction to drugs, alcohol, tobacco, gambling, or some other compulsive, uncontrollable, habitual behavior.
- Compulsive, habitual swearing and cursing.
- Fornication, adultery, homosexuality, or other compulsive sexual activity outside of marriage.
- Compulsive overspending (many people spend money to medicate their feelings of anxiety, fear, depression, or low self-worth).
- Gossip, backbiting, and destroying the reputations of others.
- Dabbling in the occult in any of its various forms: witchcraft, Wicca, neopaganism, satanism, astrology,

spiritualism, divination, tarot cards, fortune-telling, Ouija boards, and so forth.

If there is a corner of your mind, heart, or behavior that is not surrendered to Jesus Christ, that is an area where Satan will try to build a stronghold—a fortress of sin, a beachhead of ungodly thoughts and habits. There Satan will stake his claim and mark his territory, and from there he will work to expand his control over other areas of your life. Don't give Satan a stronghold from which to operate and take over even more territory in your heart and soul.

We can identify these strongholds by honest self-examination and prayer. We need to open our lives before God, holding nothing back, hiding nothing from his searching gaze. And above all, we need to pray and ask the Holy Spirit to examine us and reveal to us any stronghold that lies hidden within us. As the psalmist wrote:

> Search me, O God, and know my heart!
> Try me and know my thoughts!
> And see if there be any grievous way in me,
> and lead me in the way everlasting!
> (Psalm 139:23-24)

Strongholds cause us to fall away from grace. I'm not saying that strongholds cause us to lose our salvation, but they do cause us to neglect our spiritual abundance in Christ. Strongholds force us to live in the poverty of the struggle rather than the luxurious freedom of the grace of God. If you are spiritually living under a bridge, I want you to know that God, your heavenly Father, wants you to come home to his palace, his mansion, his paradise to enjoy all the rich freedom he offers you.

Are you aware of any strongholds in your life? Have you become aware of this issue in your life as you've been reading these pages? I believe that before you close this book, before you even finish reading this chapter, God can deliver you from these thought and behavior patterns. As Paul said, the weapons of spiritual warfare are not human weapons, but God's own power to destroy strongholds. God can demolish the spiritual strongholds in your life and set you free.

But there can be no deliverance without repentance. Many people think that repentance is saying, "Oops, sorry, Lord, I messed up again! Well, please forgive me until next time." No, repentance is the renunciation of sin. Repentance means that we renounce those strongholds in our lives and ask God to tear them down, once and for all.

The problem most of us have is that we *like* those strongholds. We're actually comfortable with those strongholds. We'd miss them if they were gone. So we don't really want God to demolish and remove those strongholds—just make them a bit more bearable.

But please understand, there can be no victory over sin unless you are willing to allow God to destroy those strongholds utterly and completely. You cannot have victory over sin while you are compromising with it. Sin must go. Strongholds must be torn down. Repentance must be complete. God must have complete control of your life.

The apostle Paul wants us to know that we can have the upper hand, we can have the victory, because Christ has set us free. When Christ is formed in you, Satan cannot come in and establish his stronghold because, as Jesus himself said, "the ruler of this world is coming. He has no claim on me" (John 14:30). The ruler of this world, at least for the time being, is Satan. And Satan has no claim on Jesus.

When Christ is formed in you, as Paul explained in Galatians 4:19, Satan can't set up housekeeping in your life. Satan can't push the temptation buzzer in your mind. Satan can't pull the sin lever in your flesh. He might have been able to at one time, but once Christ is formed in you, Jesus comes into your life and changes the combination lock—*leaving Satan out in the cold!*

So I urge you: be liberated in Christ. Enjoy the freedom and exhilaration that come with being free in him. Don't let anyone drag you into bondage to legalism or entice you into bondage to license and sin. Instead, revel in grace! Live every day in wonder and joy!

Freely, without hesitation, open up every corner of your life to God and give him complete control. That is the great paradox of the Christian life: The more you rebel against God and seek your own way, the more of a slave you become, but the more you allow God to take control of your life, the greater your freedom will be.

Bondage to sin. Liberty in Christ. Which will you choose?

8

Keeping the Supply Line Open

Galatians 5:14-26

In January 1979, our family moved from California to a rented house in Atlanta. None of us had ever seen snow before, and soon after we moved in, Atlanta experienced the worst ice storm of the century—complete with a massive power blackout.

There we were, in a strange city, knowing few people, camping out in a house without lights or power for cooking or heating water. We had no power for the electric heating system or the TV set (no news or weather reports). We huddled in that cold, dark house with our coats and blankets piled around us. We felt helpless and isolated.

That experience is a metaphor describing the spiritual condition of every person who claims to be a Christian but does not walk in the Spirit. It symbolizes the spiritual condition of everyone who does not live in the power of the Holy Spirit and who does not exhibit the fruit of the Spirit.

Every Christian possesses at least some of the *gifts* of the Spirit, but not all Christians exhibit the *fruit* of the Spirit. That is the tragedy of the church today. If you are trying to live the Christian life without the power of the Spirit and the fruit of the Spirit, you are huddled in darkness, without spiritual electricity.

The gifts of the Holy Spirit are ineffective without the fruit of the Holy Spirit.

Does that statement sound too harsh, too strong, too uncompromising to you? Then listen to what the apostle Paul tells us about the fruit of the Spirit:

> For the whole law is fulfilled in one word: "You shall love your neighbor as yourself." But if you bite and devour one another, watch out that you are not consumed by one another.
>
> But I say, walk by the Spirit, and you will not gratify the desires of the flesh. For the desires of the flesh are against the Spirit, and the desires of the Spirit are against the flesh, for these are opposed to each other, to keep you from doing the things you want to do. But if you are led by the Spirit, you are not under the law. Now the works of the flesh are evident: sexual immorality, impurity, sensuality, idolatry, sorcery, enmity, strife, jealousy, fits of anger, rivalries, dissensions, divisions, envy, drunkenness, orgies, and things like these. I warn you, as I warned you before, that those who do such things will not inherit the kingdom of God. But the fruit of the Spirit is love, joy, peace, patience, kindness, goodness, faithfulness, gentleness, self-control; against such things there is no law. And those who belong to Christ Jesus have crucified the flesh with its passions and desires.
>
> If we live by the Spirit, let us also keep in step with the Spirit. Let us not become conceited, provoking one another, envying one another (5:14-26).

Can you name the New Testament church that, more than any of its sister churches, exhibited all the gifts of the Holy Spirit? I believe that would have to be the church in Corinth. In Paul's first letter to the believers there, he wrote, "Therefore you do not lack any spiritual gift as you eagerly wait for our Lord Jesus Christ to be revealed" (1 Corinthians 1:7 NIV).

Isn't that amazing? The Corinthian church did not lack any of the spiritual gifts! When it came to gifts of the Spirit, the church in Corinth was complete. Yet immediately after affirming that these believers lacked no spiritual gifts, Paul proceeded to lecture them for their conflict and division, their tolerance of outrageous sin and immorality, their lawsuits against each other, and more. He lamented that he could not address the Corinthian believers as "people who live by the Spirit but as people who are still worldly—mere infants in Christ" (1 Corinthians 3:1 NIV).

That church, filled to overflowing with every spiritual gift, was also a hotbed of sin, corruption, conflict, and division. Next to the church in Galatia, the church in Corinth was the most messed-up church we read about in the New Testament. What was the deepest need of the church in Galatia? What was the deepest need of the Corinthian church? Both had the same urgent need: they desperately needed to exhibit the fruit of the Holy Spirit.

They had the gifts. They lacked the fruit. That is why Paul, in his famous "love chapter," 1 Corinthians 13, wrote:

> If I speak in the tongues of men and of angels, but have not love, I am a noisy gong or a clanging cymbal. And if I have prophetic powers, and understand all mysteries and all knowledge, and if I have all faith, so as to remove mountains, but have not love, I am nothing. If I give away all I have, and if I deliver up my body to be burned, but have not love, I gain nothing (1 Corinthians 13:1-3).

What is love? It is the first and most all-encompassing of the fruit of the Spirit. And Paul tells us that if we have the most miraculous and powerful and amazing gifts of the Holy Spirit, yet we lack the spiritual fruit of Christlike love, all of our amazing spiritual gifts are worth exactly nothing.

Having all the gifts of the Spirit without the fruit of the Spirit would be like owning a million-dollar Lamborghini sports car but being unable to afford gasoline. What's the point of owning the sleekest, fastest, most powerful sports car ever built if you can't even back it out of the garage?

The gifts of the Spirit are just like that Lamborghini. For fuel, you need the fruit of the Spirit. The fruit of the Spirit make the gifts of the Spirit function as God intended. If you are experiencing a power failure in your Christian life, you may have just discovered the reason why: you are missing the fruit of the Spirit.

If you don't have the fruit of the Spirit, it doesn't matter how smart you are, how rich you are, how talented you are, or how much experience you have. If you are not drawing your power from that vital source that is the Holy Spirit of God, then you are sitting helplessly in the dark, in a cold and freezing house, isolated, cut off, and helpless.

The world is full of miserable, joyless, anxious, impetuous, mean-spirited, faithless, hedonistic people. They are rude and abusive to us at work, at school, on the freeway, and over the Internet. They are sexually immoral, their language is filthy, they engage in idolatry and the occult, they blaspheme God, they are quick to start an argument, they abuse alcohol and drugs.

But the fruit of the Spirit is love, joy, peace, patience, kindness, goodness, faithfulness, gentleness, and self-control. These are the qualities that characterize the life and personality of Jesus Christ, and these are the qualities the Holy Spirit wants to build into your life.

Every Christian needs the fruit of the Spirit. Just as you cannot be saved from your sins apart from Jesus Christ, you cannot be sanctified and made Christlike apart from the work of the Holy Spirit. That is the theme of Galatians 5:14-26.

Barriers of pride and ignorance

Paul opens and closes this section of Galatians with a discussion of how Christians should relate to each other and treat each other within the church, the body of Christ. He begins by saying, "For the whole law is fulfilled in one word: 'You shall love your neighbor as yourself.' But if you bite and devour one another, watch out that you are not consumed by one another." And he closes by saying, "If we live by the Spirit, let us also keep in step with the Spirit. Let us not become conceited, provoking one another, envying one another."

The Lord is extremely concerned with how believers treat each other. Our life together as Christians must be characterized by love, the first-listed fruit of the Spirit. In the final hours before he went to the cross, Jesus prayed to the Father on behalf of his followers "that they may all be one, just as you, Father, are in me, and I in you, that they also may be in us, so that the world may believe that you have sent me" (John 17:21). As in the words of the Christian chorus, the people of this world "will know we are Christians by our love." Our oneness is our witness.

Paul also says, "But I say, walk by the Spirit, and you will not gratify the desires of the flesh. For the desires of the flesh are against the Spirit, and the desires of the Spirit are against the flesh, for these are opposed to each other, to keep you from doing the things you want to do." When we think of "the desires of the flesh," our minds immediately leap to sexual sins. But there is far more to "the desires of the flesh" than corrupted sexual desire.

The apostle Paul goes on to list "the works of the flesh," including not only sexual immorality but also idolatry, sorcery, enmity, strife, jealousy, fits of anger, rivalries, dissensions, divisions, envy, and more. Some Christians would be able to say, "I don't engage in sexual immorality"—but what Paul calls "the desires of the flesh" is a wide net that catches us all.

As we saw earlier, idols take many forms—money, fame, success, selfish ambition, pride, and more. None of us is immune from idolatry. Have you ever put your trust in good luck charms, superstitions, or horoscopes? Then you have engaged in sorcery. And who among us can claim to be completely innocent of enmity, strife, jealousy, anger, or the other fleshly sins Paul lists? All of us are guilty of the desires of the flesh.

Paul goes on to say, "But if you are led by the Spirit, you are not under the law." Throughout Paul's letter to the Galatians, we have seen him draw a stark contrast between law and grace. God gave humanity the law in order to send us all running to the arms of his grace. We are saved by grace, and the law is our tutor, our guardian, showing us that we were born in a state of illegitimacy. Grace signs our adoption papers so that we can become the beloved sons and daughters of the King.

But we mustn't stop there. Having been adopted into a royal family, we must now live up to our new status as children and heirs of the King. But how do we live up to our new station in life as royal children and heirs?

First, we must understand that we can't live up to that status in our own strength, by our own efforts. Our adopted Father invites us to draw upon his power, his strength, his resources. Our adopted Daddy wants us to plug into his infinite power source and no longer live in a state of darkness, a state of power failure.

Please understand, only two things can keep you from plugging into God's infinite power. Only two things will keep you from living a Spirit-filled life. Those two things are *pride* and *ignorance*.

Prideful Christians try to live up to their royal status through their own efforts. They are too proud to admit they can't live godly lives in their own strength. And ignorant Christians try to live up to their royal status through their own efforts because they don't understand how to access the power of God by his Spirit.

To all of us who pridefully, ignorantly try and fail to be worthy of our royal status, Paul says, "But I say, walk by the Spirit, and you will not gratify the desires of the flesh." This is a profound statement. In the original Greek language, it is stated in the present tense and imperative mood. This means Paul is telling us that walking by the Spirit is not something we do once and for all. It is a continuous action. He is telling us, "Keep on walking and walking and walking by the Spirit—and if you do that, you will not fall prey to the desires of the flesh."

Walking implies progress. If you are walking by the Spirit, you will see spiritual progress in your life. You will see growth taking place—maybe not from one day to the next, but certainly from year to year in your Christian life. At the end of each year, you should be able to look back at where you were a year ago and say, "God has been changing me, teaching me, leading me, and helping me to grow. I'm not the same person I was a year ago. What a difference the Holy Spirit is making in my life!"

The fruit of the Spirit

This brings us to the central theme of this passage: the fruit of the Spirit. What is the evidence that demonstrates we are making spiritual progress in our lives? The fruit of the Spirit. How do we acquire the fruit of the Spirit? By walking by the Spirit. The fruit of the Spirit is manifested when we have yielded our lives to the control of the Holy Spirit.

Yielding to the Spirit is a decision of the will. You can't simply rest on your blessed assurance and say, "I want to be filled by the Spirit of God today." If that were possible, Paul would not have given us the command to "walk."

Walking is action. Walking by the Spirit is taking action by the Spirit and being led and controlled by the Spirit. To walk by the Spirit, you can't sit on the sidelines. You can't straddle the fence. You can't be indifferent. You can't remain neutral. You can't say, "I'm just waiting for the Spirit to fill me." You have to *walk*.

Paul also tells us that the Christian life is a form of warfare. It's a fight, a battle. He writes, "For the desires of the flesh are against the Spirit, and the desires of the Spirit are against the flesh, for these are opposed to each other, to keep you from doing the things you want to do."

In spiritual warfare, there are only two kinds of people—victors and victims. You are either a winner or a loser. You are numbered among the quick or the dead. But know this: When you walk by the Spirit, you are assured of victory. When you are led by the Spirit and controlled by the Spirit, you cannot lose.

But if you ignore Paul's urgent call to walk in the Spirit, if you try to live the Christian life by your own efforts, according to your own limited wisdom, you can count on defeat. Satan and the flesh will eat your lunch.

Think of the spiritual life and the fleshly life as two dogs in your yard. The spiritual life as a proud and noble breed; the fleshly life is a mangy, ugly mongrel. You can feed only one or the other. Which one will you feed? Which one will you starve? The one you feed will grow. The one you starve will die.

God calls you to feed the spiritual life and starve the fleshly life.

If you yield your life to the Spirit of God, your spiritual life will grow strong and healthy, and the desires of the flesh will wither and die.

Many people have the common misunderstanding that when Paul refers to the desires of the flesh, he is saying there is something sinful and unwholesome about the physical body. That's not what Paul is saying. The human body is not intrinsically sinful. God created the human body as a thing of beauty, "fearfully and wonderfully made," as the psalmist has said (Psalm 139:14). The human body is an instrument, a "house" we inhabit during our earthly sojourn. It is morally neutral.

When the Bible speaks about "the flesh," it is using a metaphor or symbol that stands for all the sinful desires that assault our bodies. "The flesh" stands for our gluttonous desires, our immoral sexual desires, our greed and lusts, our pride and selfish ambition, our envy and strife, our bitterness and hate—all of these sinful desires are involved in what Paul calls "the flesh."

When the Holy Spirit controls the body, when you are walking in the Spirit, then the Spirit will give you victory over the desires of the flesh. But if the flesh controls the body, then you will feed those fleshly desires—and I can predict with certainty that you will experience consequences from feeding the flesh: anxiety, guilt, fear, worry, and more.

I once heard about a businessman who was thinking of buying a rundown warehouse property. As he walked through the building with his real estate agent, he could see that the warehouse had been vacant for months and was in serious need of repair.

"Vandals smashed those windows and ripped out that door," the real estate agent said. "But with just a few repairs and a new coat of paint, this old building won't look so bad."

"I'll buy it," the businessman said, "but I won't repair it. I don't want the building. I want this site. I'm going to build a brand-new building here."

We human beings are just like that real estate agent. All we can envision for our lives is fixing things up, making repairs, adding a new coat of paint to hide the defects, and doing it all in our own strength.

But God is like that businessman. He's not interested in making a few repairs so that we "won't look so bad." He is in the business of making all things new. All he wants from us is the site—and our permission for him to knock down the old and start building the new.

So it is with all those who are born of the Spirit of God. When you received Jesus Christ as your Lord and Savior, you were born again, you were born by the Spirit. The Holy Spirit came into your life. Does every Christian who is born of the Spirit also *yield* to the Spirit? Some do and some don't.

Some Christians, either because of pride or ignorance, are reluctant to yield to the Spirit immediately. As a result, the Spirit does not fill them, so they live a fleshly life. They may try to make a few repairs in their own strength so they "won't look so bad" as Christians. But the old flesh, the old man, still dominates their lives.

We see this principle in the life of the Corinthian church and the Galatian churches. The Christians in these churches were born again by the Spirit of God. Paul tells us that very clearly in his letters to those churches. But the believers in those churches, out of pride and ignorance, had failed to yield their lives to the control of the Holy Spirit. As a result, the Corinthian and Galatian churches were torn by division, strife, and immorality.

In the Corinthian church, the problem was primarily ignorance. The Christians in Corinth lacked an understanding of the importance of Christian love, unity, and purity in the life of the church. Out of their ignorance, they failed to yield themselves to the Holy

Spirit. As a result, the Corinthian Christians either committed or tolerated immorality in their midst. So Paul had to write to them to cure them of their ignorance.

In the Galatian church, the problem was pride. The Galatian Christians pridefully chose to live a legalistic lifestyle, trying to earn their salvation by their own efforts. Until you yield control of your life to the Spirit of God, you are living in pride. You are trying to construct your own means of salvation rather than accepting the grace God makes available to you by faith in Jesus Christ alone.

As human beings we tend to make doctrine based on our personal experience instead of the objective truth of the Word of God. Some people come to Christ with a sense of excitement and intensity, and they immediately yield themselves to the Holy Spirit and experience the Spirit-filled life. As a result, they tend to believe that all Christians should experience the filling of the Holy Spirit one time, at the beginning of their Christian walk, and that one experience carries them throughout their Christian life.

Other Christians come to Christ but don't immediately yield every corner of their lives to the control of the Holy Spirit. They go on living as carnal Christians for months or years. Then, at some point, they come under the conviction of the Holy Spirit, and they begin to yield their lives to him. In the process, they experience even more joy and excitement in the Lord. So they invent a "doctrine" based on their experience, claiming there are two stages in the Christian walk.

Neither view deserves the status of a doctrine. Neither is right or wrong in every case.

The Bible is clear: Whenever you willingly choose to yield to the Holy Spirit, the Spirit will come and indwell you. Whenever you willingly surrender to the Spirit of God, he will take control of your life and give you victory. Whenever you willingly let go of your spiritual pride and stop trying to please God by your own efforts, the Spirit will fill you to overflowing, and you will experience the fruit of the Spirit, including the joy of the Spirit. As the apostle Paul wrote to the Christians in Rome:

> For those who live according to the flesh set their minds on the things of the flesh, but those who live according to the Spirit set their minds on the things of the Spirit. For to set the mind on the flesh is death, but to set the mind on the Spirit is life and peace. For the mind that is set on the flesh is hostile to God, for it does not submit to God's law; indeed, it cannot. Those who are in the flesh cannot please God (Romans 8:5-8).

Paul tells us in our Galatians 5 passage, "Now the works of the flesh are evident: sexual immorality, impurity, sensuality, idolatry, sorcery, enmity, strife, jealousy, fits of anger, rivalries, dissensions, divisions, envy, drunkenness, orgies, and things like these. I warn you, as I warned you before, that those who do such things will not inherit the kingdom of God" (5:19-21). Bear in mind this is only a partial list!

When it comes to sinning, we human beings are endlessly creative. We are constantly coming up with new ways to sin against God and each other. For example, many people today combine the age-old sin of sexual immorality with the latest cell phone texting technology to come up with "sexting."

If you claim to be a Spirit-filled Christian, yet you are living in sin—whether one of Paul's listed sins or an unlisted one—your claim is not believable. If you claim to be Spirit-filled, yet you are practicing adultery, fornication, or homosexuality, who are you fooling? If you claim to be Spirit-filled, yet you engage in substance abuse (street drugs, prescription medications, or "medical marijuana"), it's not the Spirit of God that controls your life. If you claim to be Spirit-filled, yet you are gossiping, destroying reputations, stirring up dissension and division, and prone to angry outbursts, then I'm sorry, but it's not the Spirit of God that fills you, it's a spirit of bitterness and envy.

Jesus himself gave us a similar list of sins that emanate from within: "What comes out of a person is what defiles him. For from within, out of the heart of man, come evil thoughts, sexual immorality, theft, murder, adultery, coveting, wickedness, deceit, sensuality, envy, slander, pride, foolishness. All these evil things come from within, and they defile a person" (Mark 7:20-23).

What is inside of us inevitably comes out. You can't get drinking water from an oil well. If you are filled with the Spirit of God, godliness will flow from your life. If you are filled with evil thoughts, sexual immorality, theft, murder, adultery, and other fleshly things, that is what will flow from your life.

You are either filled with the Spirit or you are filled with the works of the flesh. There is no third substance, no third alternative.

Please understand, I'm not saying that a Spirit-filled Christian can live a sinless life. There will be moments when we give in to the temptation of lust or envy, moments when we yield to anger or strife. There will be times when we become embroiled in dissension and disputes that might not even be our fault—misunderstandings do happen.

But if there are stubborn patterns of sinful thoughts and sinful behavior in your life, then you have to ask yourself, *On what basis do I call myself a Christian? Where is the evidence that the Holy Spirit fills me and controls my life? If I were arrested for being a Christian, would there be enough evidence to convict me?*

If you honestly examine yourself and conclude that you have not yielded your life to the Spirit of God, if you have to conclude that you are not a Spirit-filled Christian, then you should ask yourself if you were ever truly born again in the first place. As the apostle Paul continues in his letter to the Romans:

> You, however, are not in the flesh but in the Spirit, if in fact the Spirit of God dwells in you. Anyone who does not have the Spirit of Christ does not belong to him (Romans 8:9).

If, on honest self-examination, you have to question whether your life reveals any evidence of Spirit-filling, then I urge you to consider this question very seriously: Do you truly belong to Christ or not?

Christlikeness is the goal

In Galatians 5:22-24, we come to the crux of this passage. This is the yardstick with which we measure our spiritual maturity. Here Paul introduces to us the fruit of the Spirit:

> But the fruit of the Spirit is love, joy, peace, patience, kindness, goodness, faithfulness, gentleness, self-control; against such things there is no law. And those who belong to Christ Jesus have crucified the flesh with its passions and desires.

What Paul calls "the fruit of the Spirit" consists of nine traits or character qualities that characterize the mature and Spirit-filled follower of Christ. The nine fruit of the Spirit are grouped in threes.

The first group of three—love, joy, and peace—are qualities that grow in our lives as a result of our relationship with God. Bible commentator Warren Wiersbe puts it this way: "The first three qualities express the *Godward* aspect of the Christian life."[13] The Spirit of God fills our hearts with *agape* love, divine love, a love that God plants in our hearts, transcending mere emotions. The Spirit also plants *joy* in our hearts—a sense of God's sufficiency that transcends our circumstances. And the Spirit also plants *peace* in our hearts—the peace that transcends human understanding (Philippians 4:7).

The second group of three—patience, kindness, and goodness—are qualities we demonstrate in our relationships with others. Wiersbe writes, "The next three express the *manward* aspect of the Christian life."[14] *Patience* is also known as endurance—a refusal to quit. Spirit-filled Christians persevere in their relationships with others and refuse to give up on others. *Kindness* is the quality of treating others gently, mercifully, and lovingly. *Goodness* is the quality of trying to create an atmosphere of godliness, righteousness, and fairness in our dealings with others.

The third group of three—faithfulness, gentleness, and self-control—are qualities we demonstrate in our inner being and our private moments. Wiersbe observes, "The final three qualities are *selfward*."[15] These qualities describe the Spirit-filled Christian who is consistent, *faithful*, and dependable, even when no one else is looking. He or she has the trait of *gentleness*—not weakness, but strength under control. And the Spirit-filled Christian possesses *self-control*—a quality of being self-disciplined, self-regulated, and self-governing. A person who is self-controlled never needs to be controlled by others.

So the fruit of the Spirit can be divided into three categories—the Godward fruit, the manward fruit, and the selfward fruit.

A number of years ago, I had a conversation with a famous, successful man. As we talked, he opened up his life and feelings to me and confessed that he was frustrated, angry, and full of bitter hatred because of wounds he had suffered earlier in his life.

So I opened my Bible and read to him the fruit of the Spirit from Galatians 5:22. Then I said, "Is this what you are looking for?"

The man began to sob. "Yes," he said. "Yes, that is my deepest need."

He was right. The fruit of the Spirit is not only his deepest need, but the deepest need of every human soul. You cannot purchase the fruit of the Spirit with all the money in the world. You cannot achieve the fruit of the Spirit through your own efforts, even if you work at it day and night. You cannot manufacture the fruit of the Spirit no matter how hard you try.

People sometimes refer to these nine spiritual qualities as "the fruits of the Spirit." But *fruit* is singular, not plural. These nine qualities are not a basket of assorted fruits but a cluster of fruit, a collective noun. God fills your life with the fruit of the Spirit when you yield every last inch of your life to the Holy Spirit of God, nothing held back. He loves you and wants to fill your life to overflowing.

It's important to notice, too, what the fruit of the Spirit adds up to. When you look at these nine qualities, this cluster of fruit, a picture emerges. *It's a picture of Jesus.*

After all, who is the one person you know who is always loving, joyful, and full of peace? Who is the one person you know who is always patient, kind, and full of goodness? Who is the one person you know who is always faithful, gentle, and self-controlled? Who is the one person you know who expresses all of these qualities in full measure and in perfect harmony?

There is only one answer. There is only one person. There is only one Jesus.

When you yield your life to the Spirit of God, and the Holy Spirit comes in and fills you, he will produce in you the life and character of the Lord Jesus Christ. To put it in the terms of Galatians 4:19, Christ will be formed in you. Or in the terms of Romans 8:29, you will be conformed into the image of Christ.

Christlikeness is the goal of our lives, the goal of our Christian walk. And the fruit of the Spirit is the evidence of Christlikeness in our lives.

Crucify the flesh!

Paul concludes his discussion of the works of the flesh versus the fruit of the Spirit with this statement: "And those who belong to Christ Jesus have crucified the flesh with its passions and desires" (5:24). He is saying that, just as Jesus Christ was crucified on the cross, so you and I must crucify the flesh every single day of our lives.

If you want to be like Jesus, if you want to have Christ formed in you, then the first act you perform each day must be the act of hammering nails into the desires of the flesh. And the hammer you use is not the hammer of your own human effort, but the hammer of the Holy Spirit. You crucify the desires of the flesh by consciously, willingly going to God in prayer and saying, *Lord, I give you control of my life. I hold nothing back from you. Crucify everything that is evil within me. Let me be conformed to your likeness more and more each day.*

John R. W. Stott gave us a tremendous insight into what it means to crucify the flesh with its passions and desires. He pointed out three aspects of crucifixion that we must apply to our lives in order to crucify the flesh.

First, *crucifixion was always executed without pity for the condemned.* So when you crucify your flesh, with its passions and desires, you must show the flesh no mercy. "If, therefore, we are to 'crucify' our flesh," Stott wrote, "it is plain that the flesh is not something respectable to be treated with courtesy and deference, but something so evil that it deserves no better fate than to be crucified."[16]

Second, *crucifixion is incredibly painful.* So crucifying the flesh will be painful as well. We tend to be weak and soft where pain is concerned, and the very thought of having to do something painful strikes us as grossly unfair. But it was grossly unfair for Jesus to go to the cross on your behalf and mine. How much comfort are you willing to sacrifice, how many sinful pleasures are you willing to forego, how much pain are you willing to accept in order to crucify the flesh and demonstrate your gratitude to the Lord Jesus? Yes, crucifixion is painful, but God will give you his peace and joy in the midst of the pain.

Third, *crucifixion is decisive.* "Although death by crucifixion was a lingering death," Stott wrote, "it was a certain death...If we [have] crucified the flesh, we must leave it there to die. We must renew every day this attitude towards sin of ruthless and uncompromising rejection."[17]

In reliance on God, under the control of the Holy Spirit, we can break the hold of the flesh on our lives. We do not have to be dominated by the flesh, with its passions and desires. "If we live by the Spirit," Paul concludes, "let us also keep in step with the Spirit. Let us not become conceited, provoking one another, envying one another."

Don't be content to live out your Christian life in the darkness of a power failure. Don't accept a lifetime of huddling and shivering in the cold. Plug in to the power of the Holy Spirit and let him fill you with his warmth and light today—and for the rest of your life.

9

The Law of Sowing and Reaping

Galatians 6

Years ago, I heard the story of two teenagers, both seniors in high school, who were going out on a date. The young man called at the door for his girlfriend, and he chatted with the parents for a few minutes until their daughter came downstairs. The girl's mother thought she caught some secret signal pass from her daughter to the young man, and she wondered, *What did* that *mean?*

The couple left—but the girl's mother could not get her daughter's little gesture out of her mind. As she and her husband went to bed that night, she couldn't sleep.

She was still tossing and turning at nearly midnight when the phone rang. It was the police. The daughter and her boyfriend had been in a car crash. The girl was seriously hurt—and the young man was dead.

The parents rushed to the hospital. There they learned that their daughter would live, but with permanent scars. They also learned that both the daughter and her boyfriend had been drinking. A half-empty bottle was found in the car.

"If I ever find out who gave liquor to those kids," the father said in a cold rage, "I'll kill him!"

The parents eventually returned home in the early hours of the morning. They were exhausted and emotionally drained but too shaken to sleep. The father went to the liquor cabinet for a drink to "take the edge off." When he opened the cabinet, he found a note that his daughter had written, left in place of a missing bottle. The note read something like this: "Dad, if you find this note, please don't be mad. We just borrowed a bottle to have a good time. Love you. XOXOX."

It's not easy to be a parent today. It's not easy to get our kids to listen to our advice, to follow our guidance, to accept our beliefs and our values. But by far the most difficult and challenging task of parenting is to set an example for our child to emulate.

Children need to be instructed and taught. We need to talk to them continually about faith, values, virtues, and life lessons, but the greatest influence our children will ever know is the influence of our *example*.

All too many times I have heard parents say (with shocking casualness), "What can I do? I don't have any influence with my kids anymore. They just need to sow their wild oats."

There's an obvious flaw in that kind of thinking. The flaw is that people reap what they sow. Anyone who sows wild oats can expect to reap a harvest of sorrow and shame—and maybe worse.

I've never met anyone who has planted a crop of wild oats, then looked back years later and said, "I'm so glad I did that. I'm so glad I did my share of alcohol and drugs, partying and one-night stands. I'm sure glad I had the wisdom not to pass up those wild oats." But

I've met literally thousands of people who have shared their regrets, wept over their bad choices, and lamented their guilt feelings and the consequences of what they have sown.

There is a basic, universal, inviolable law of spiritual agriculture: It is foolish to sow wild oats, then pray for crop failure. We all reap what we sow. That is a lesson we need to teach relentlessly to our children.

Restoring one another in a spirit of gentleness

As we come to the last chapter of Paul's letter to the Galatians, we see that Paul gathers all of his arguments into a grand conclusion, and his central theme focuses on the biblical principle of sowing and reaping. Paul wants us to know that some things that people repeatedly, irrationally try to do simply cannot be done.

We cannot sow bad habits, then reap a good character. We cannot sow jealousy and hatred, then reap love and friendship. We cannot sow self-destructive behavior, then reap a healthy body. We cannot sow deception and hypocrisy, then reap trust and loyalty. We cannot sow timidity and cowardice, then reap confidence and courage. We cannot sow neglect for God's Word, then reap a victorious life.

Paul opens Galatians 6 with wise, practical counsel on how we should sow kindness and support for one another in the church, the body of Christ:

> Brothers, if anyone is caught in any transgression, you who are spiritual should restore him in a spirit of gentleness. Keep watch on yourself, lest you too be tempted (6:1).

The apostle tells us that we have a responsibility toward one another as Christians. And one of our responsibilities, if we are spiritually mature, is to gently, humbly restore the fallen Christian. Here's an apt analogy: Suppose you see a person stumble and fall, and that person needs to get up but can't get up without help. What should you do? Clearly, you would help that person.

Paul carefully chooses the phrase "caught in any transgression" to describe this situation. He's not talking about someone who is a deliberate, habitual sinner, but someone who has essentially been "caught off guard" and has "stumbled" into sin. This is probably a person who flirted with temptation, thinking he would not fall—but he was wrong. Perhaps he was trying to live the Christian life by his own effort instead of being filled with the Spirit.

The apostle wants us to know that we, as believers who are walking in the Spirit, filled with the Spirit, and manifesting the fruit of the Spirit, have a responsibility toward fellow believers who have stumbled. By virtue of our spiritual strength, we have a duty toward those who are going through a time of spiritual weakness. We are responsible for those who have been snared by the flesh, with its passions and desires.

So this is our duty—to restore our fellow believers in a spirit of gentleness. The original Greek word translated "restore" is a medical term that refers to setting a broken bone or putting a dislocated limb back into joint. We who are walking in the Spirit and led by the Spirit are to help fallen believers who have been wounded by the passions and desires of the flesh.

The first step in helping fallen believers is to help them to recognize their sin as sin. Sometimes fallen believers refuse help because they are in denial about their sin. Until a person admits his sin, he cannot be helped and restored.

But Paul is careful to point out that we who are spiritual need to approach those who have fallen in a spirit of gentleness and humility. We must be aware that we, too, could easily fall into a similar sin. No one is immune to the lure of the flesh. Next time, you or I could be in need of gentle restoration.

Notice how Paul's counsel here relates to his counsel in Galatians 5 regarding the fruit of the Spirit. Gentleness is part of that cluster of fruit. If we catch someone in a sin and try to restore that person in a spirit of harshness or condemnation, if we behave in a self-righteous or condescending way, it's unlikely that we'll succeed. When people are confronted harshly, they feel attacked. When attacked, their defenses go up. You cannot restore someone who feels defensive. But you can restore someone who feels cared for, supported, and loved. That's why a spirit of gentleness is so important.

Calvin Coolidge was the thirtieth president of the United States. Early in his presidency, he was away from the White House, staying in a hotel. He woke up in his hotel room to find a young man—a burglar—going through the pockets of his trousers.

"Young man," he said to the startled burglar, "you may have my watch, but please leave the watch chain. There is a charm on the chain that has sentimental value."

Then President Coolidge engaged the young man in conversation. It turned out that the would-be thief didn't even know that the hotel room was occupied by the president. He was a college student, down on his luck, trying to scrape together enough money for a train ticket back to college. He told the president he had never stolen before.

"Would you please hand me my wallet?" the president asked. The young man handed Coolidge his wallet. Coolidge counted out $32, the price of the ticket, and handed the cash to the young man. "This is a loan. I know you'll pay it back. Now, I suggest you leave by the window, the same way you came in. There are Secret Service men in the hallway, and I think it would be best if you did not meet them."

The young man left. A few weeks later, President Coolidge received a letter of thanks from the young man, along with the repayment of the loan. That's what it means to restore someone in a spirit of gentleness.

All too often, when someone in the church is caught in a transgression, others in the church take the matter to the "prayer circle." Intercessory prayer is a good thing, of course, and the church needs more of it—but I have also seen Christians use prayer as an excuse for gossip. One person gets on the phone, calls a number of praying friends, spreads a word of evil gossip, then concludes with those five pious words that are supposed to transform the sin of gossip into a sacrament: "We must pray for them."

Gossip is a sinful and destructive response when someone is caught in a transgression. But there is another response that is equally sinful and destructive: indifference. That's when we hear that someone is caught in a transgression, and we respond, "That's none of my business. I don't want to get involved."

There is only one truly spiritual and Spirit-led response when we learn that someone is caught in a transgression: We must restore that person with gentleness—and we should do so only after a great deal of prayer and self-examination, especially an examination of our motives.

I can remember occasions when I have felt the Lord tugging at my heart, urging me to go to someone who was caught in a transgression. I have never been eager to go. It's always a painful burden to have to address sin in the life of another brother or sister in Christ. On those occasions, I ask God to search my heart and purify my motives, and then I go to that person—and almost every time, I go with tears in my eyes.

Why do these encounters make me so emotional? In part, it's because I feel a great sorrow and sadness for the person I have to talk to. But even more so, I have tears in my eyes because I am conscious of my frailty, my weaknesses, and my vulnerability to sin. As

I look at the other person, I can't help thinking, *There but for the grace of God go I.*

It's painful and emotionally exhausting to talk to others about their sin, and those who are spiritual will be reluctant to shoulder the burden. But those who are led and controlled by the Spirit will restore that person in a spirit of gentleness.

Remember, in Genesis 4, after Cain murdered his brother Abel, the Lord asked Cain where his brother was. Cain replied, "Am I my brother's keeper?" Paul, in Galatians 6:1, wants us to know that the answer to that question is yes.

How to fulfill the law of Christ

Next, Paul writes:

> Bear one another's burdens, and so fulfill the law of Christ. For if anyone thinks he is something, when he is nothing, he deceives himself. But let each one test his own work, and then his reason to boast will be in himself alone and not in his neighbor. For each will have to bear his own load (6:2-5).

Here, Paul returns to the central theme of Galatians—grace and Spirit versus the law. He contrasts a Spirit-filled Christian with a legalist. Spirit-filled Christians are always ready to bear one another's burdens; legalists are always eager to add to the burdens of others.

God placed us in a family of faith, a body of believers, for a reason. He knew that Christians should not have to bear their burdens alone, but should have brothers and sisters to call upon for help and encouragement. When we help to bear the burdens and lighten the load of our fellow Christians, we fulfill the law of Christ—the command to love one another.

The apostle Paul experienced great adversity, anxiety, and discouragement in his ministry, yet he also experienced encouragement from fellow believers who helped him to bear his burdens. He once wrote, "For even when we came into Macedonia, our bodies had no rest, but we were afflicted at every turn—fighting without and fear within. But God, who comforts the downcast, comforted us by the coming of Titus" (2 Corinthians 7:5-6).

Every once in a while, we all need a Titus in our lives—someone to help us shoulder the burdens that weigh us down. And every once in a while, God calls each of us to become a Titus in the life of another struggling believer. Who is the Titus in your life right now? And who is the apostle Paul in your life, whose burden you are helping to carry?

Some people are confused by the fact that Paul says, "Bear one another's burdens," then, just a few verses later, he adds, "For each will have to bear his own load." Isn't this a contradiction? No. Again, it's important to remember that Paul is contrasting grace versus law. As people who live by grace and Christlike love, we bear one another's burdens as an act of love.

What do legalists do? They are constantly interfering in the lives of others, adding to their burden, and making other people miserable with their long lists of dos and don'ts. Spirit-led Christians lift the burdens of others. Legalists don't lift the burdens of others—they *add* to the burdens of others.

As Jesus himself said, legalists such as the scribes, Pharisees, and Judaizers "tie up heavy burdens, hard to bear, and lay them on people's shoulders, but they themselves are not willing to move them with their finger" (Matthew 23:4).

Here in Galatians 6, Paul tells the legalists, in effect, "Stop adding to the burdens of other Christians. Stop sticking your legalistic nose in other people's business. Test your own good works and make sure you are living up to your legalistic standards before inflicting them on someone else. When you give an account for your life, God will not ask about your neighbor's actions. You'll be judged for the way you've lived your own life. So don't fool yourself into thinking you're holy when you're not."

When most people see someone struggling to carry a heavy box or suitcase, a natural human emotion of caring and concern takes over. We drop what we're doing and go help that person. But some people in this world—and yes, some of them are in the church—simply lack compassion, mercy, and Christlike grace. When they see someone struggling with a burden, whether physical, emotional, or spiritual, they are unmoved. They think it's beneath their dignity to lift a finger to help others.

Paul speaks of such people when he writes, "For if anyone thinks he is something, when he is nothing, he deceives himself" (6:3). If you won't stoop to lift a fellow Christian's burden, if you think it is beneath your dignity to show mercy to others, then you are self-deceived. You have an inflated opinion of yourself.

That's why Paul commands us to not compare ourselves with others. God does not grade us on a curve. He grades our lives by his objective standard of righteousness. We will have to give an account for our own actions, not the actions of others. So let's stop comparing ourselves to others and start shouldering one another's burden—and so fulfill the law of Christ.

Conduct shapes character

Paul goes on to explain how we should sow the seed of holy living and serving others:

> Let the one who is taught the word share all good things with the one who teaches. Do not be deceived: God is not mocked, for whatever one sows, that will he

also reap. For the one who sows to his own flesh will from the flesh reap corruption, but the one who sows to the Spirit will from the Spirit reap eternal life. And let us not grow weary of doing good, for in due season we will reap, if we do not give up. So then, as we have opportunity, let us do good to everyone, and especially to those who are of the household of faith (6:6-10).

If a farmer wants to reap a harvest, he must cultivate the soil and sow the seed. And if he wants to harvest corn, he needs to plant corn, not some other seed. If he plants wheat, he should not expect to harvest a crop of corn. And if he wants to reap a rich, plentiful harvest of corn, he should plant generously, not sparingly, and he should sow good seed, not bad.

These principles hold true in the spiritual realm just as in the agricultural realm. Many twenty-first-century Christians find these principles hard to accept, and even hard to understand. We're accustomed to instant results, instant gratification, and instant solutions to long-term problems.

Overweight? Slim down fast with this miracle diet pill! Or faster yet, have this surgical procedure. The idea of dieting, exercising, and becoming more self-disciplined seems too hard, requires too much patience, and simply takes too long.

The principle of sowing and reaping, of working patiently until the harvest, is alien to our experience. Most of us have no idea what it takes to produce the food we eat. We go to the market and the food magically lines the shelves. Or if we are *really* in a hurry, we go to any fast-food restaurant and have our food served to us mere seconds after we place our order.

So this spiritual concept of sowing and reaping makes little sense to us. It does not relate to our everyday experience. But this is God's truth for our lives: Sowing and reaping require time and patience.

The farmer doesn't simply scatter the seed one day, then go out the next day and dig up the ground to see how his plants are progressing. There are seasons of seed time and harvest, and these cannot be rushed.

If you sow good seed in the ground of your life, if you nurture it and water it with prayer and God's Word, if you are patient and obedient, then you can expect to reap a spiritual bumper crop. If you sow seeds of obedience, prayer, and Scripture meditation, you will be blessed with the fruit of the Spirit. If you sow seeds of kindness and love, you will be blessed with a harvest of friends. If you sow seeds of tithes and offerings to God, you will be blessed with a financial harvest, and your needs will be met.

Paul adds, "Do not be deceived: God is not mocked." In other words, don't sneer at God, don't try to outwit God, don't think you can violate his principles with impunity. "For," Paul continues, "whatever one sows, that will he also reap. For the one who sows to his own flesh will from the flesh reap corruption, but the one who sows to the Spirit will from the Spirit reap eternal life" (6:7-8).

The Christian life is a battleground, and the flesh is constantly at war with the Spirit for control of our lives. The choices you make will determine who wins that war—the flesh or the Spirit. What you sow determines what you reap. You and I are not helpless victims of our circumstances. We choose whether to live holy, pure lives—and therefore, we choose whether to experience a life of peace and joy or a life of shame and regret.

Our character is shaped by our conduct. And our conduct is shaped by our choices. The old adage is true: "Sow a thought, reap an action; sow an action, reap a habit; sow a habit, reap a character; sow a character, reap a destiny." This maxim embraces biblical truth. It's another way of saying that if you sow to the flesh, you will reap corruption, and if you sow to the Spirit, you will reap eternal life.

Next, Paul transitions from sowing and reaping in the realm of personal holiness to sowing and reaping in the lives of others:

> And let us not grow weary of doing good, for in due season we will reap, if we do not give up. So then, as we have opportunity, let us do good to everyone, and especially to those who are of the household of faith (6:9-10).

Christianity is not a spectator sport. Everyone is expected to be in the game. Every believer is a minister of God's grace, of the good news of Jesus Christ. So if you are an active and obedient Christian, if you are actively involved in ministry and witnessing to others, you will face times of temptation and discouragement. There will be moments when you wish you could simply give up, moments when it seems that the Christian life is not worth the adversity, the persecution, the exhaustion, and the soul-weariness.

I have faced this enemy called discouragement many times, and I know you have as well. It is discouraging to preach your heart out from the book of Galatians, to expose the dangers of legalism, to exalt the wonders of God's grace—and then to turn right around and see seemingly mature Christians haggling and fighting with each other over legalistic nonessentials.

And Satan will take advantage of those times of discouragement. He will whisper, "You're wasting your breath. Not a soul is listening. You might as easily flap your wings and fly to the moon as persuade people to follow Christ and grow in him."

Sometimes the whisperings of Satan seem to make more sense to our limited understanding than the commands of God. Don't let Satan bring you down or hold you back. Don't grow weary of doing good for God. Refuse to give up! Keep on sowing, keep doing God's will, keep doing good toward those who are in the church and those who are on the outside—and you will reap an everlasting harvest.

Written in large letters

In the concluding verses of Galatians, Paul issues a gracious benediction and a final warning—and he underscores these closing words in a unique way:

> See with what large letters I am writing to you with my own hand. It is those who want to make a good showing in the flesh who would force you to be circumcised, and only in order that they may not be persecuted for the cross of Christ. For even those who are circumcised do not themselves keep the law, but they desire to have you circumcised that they may boast in your flesh. But far be it from me to boast except in the cross of our Lord Jesus Christ, by which the world has been crucified to me, and I to the world. For neither circumcision counts for anything, nor uncircumcision, but a new creation. And as for all who walk by this rule, peace and mercy be upon them, and upon the Israel of God.
>
> From now on let no one cause me trouble, for I bear on my body the marks of Jesus.
>
> The grace of our Lord Jesus Christ be with your spirit, brothers. Amen (6:11-18).

In these closing words, Paul returns to the theme of our Christian liberty, and he writes of sowing seeds of freedom and grace. Notice especially Paul's words in verse 16: "And as for all who walk by this rule, peace and mercy be upon them, and upon the Israel of God." The phrase "all who walk by this rule" refers to all who are saved by grace through faith, and not by keeping the ceremonial law. And the phrase "the Israel of God" refers to the church of Jesus Christ.

As I stand in the Reformed tradition, I believe that the church, the new Israel of God, is made up of all the Old Testament saints who looked *forward* by faith to the cross, and all the New Testament saints who look *backward* to the cross. We see this principle throughout the New Testament. We are heirs of Abraham; therefore, God's promises to Abraham now apply to us.

For example, the apostle Peter writes, "But you are a chosen race, a royal priesthood, a holy nation, a people for his own possession, that you may proclaim the excellencies of him who called you out of darkness into his marvelous light" (1 Peter 2:9). Those phrases—"a chosen race, a royal priesthood, a holy nation, a people for his own possession"—were used in the Old Testament to describe the nation of Israel (see Exodus 19:5-6; Deuteronomy 7:6, 14:2; 1 Kings 3:8). Now Peter applies these same phrases to the church of Jesus Christ.

The apostle Paul agrees with Peter, telling us that God's promises to Israel now apply to the church—that is, to every person, Jew or Gentile, who trusts in Jesus as Lord and Savior. In Romans 2:28-29a, Paul writes, "For no one is a Jew who is merely one outwardly, nor is circumcision outward and physical. But a Jew is one inwardly, and circumcision is a matter of the heart, by the Spirit, not by the letter." And in Galatians 3:29, he writes, "And if you are Christ's, then you are Abraham's offspring, heirs according to promise."

So the promises God made to Abraham and to Israel now apply to "the Israel of God," the church of Jesus Christ. Does this mean that God has now excluded Israel from the promise or that he has washed his hands of the Jewish people? Absolutely not! The nation of Israel is still ground zero of God's plan for human history. The Jewish people are still welcomed into "the Israel of God" on the same basis they have always been, in both the Old and New Testaments: "everyone who calls on the name of the LORD shall be saved," and "the righteous shall live by his faith" (see Joel 2:32 and Habakkuk 2:4).

Throughout this letter, Paul has been dictating his thoughts to an amanuensis, a person who takes dictation and writes down Paul's thoughts. But here, in these final verses, Paul takes the pen from the hand of the scribe, and he doesn't merely sign his name, as is the usual custom. He writes the final paragraphs in his own hand.

"See with what large letters I am writing to you with my own hand," he writes (6:11). Some have speculated that he wrote with enlarged letters because he had poor eyesight. Others have suggested that he wrote with large letters for emphasis. Whatever the reason for his large letters, in these final verses, Paul circled back to his original theme: the secret power of the Christian life. True power for Christian living does not come from the outside, through external rituals and actions. True power is an inward manifestation of the filling of the Holy Spirit and the liberating grace of God.

The more legalistic a person is, the less spiritual he is. The more external your faith is, the less likely you will have a vibrant internal relationship with the living God.

Take it from Paul. He knew the life of a cold-hearted legalistic Pharisee, and he knew the life of a liberated, grace-oriented follower of Christ. He had experienced both the deadly rituals of the law and the liberating Spirit of grace. His message to us is: "For neither circumcision counts for anything, nor uncircumcision, but a new creation" (6:15).

In other words, it doesn't matter if a religious symbol has been cut into your flesh or not. All that matters is whether you are a new creation. As Paul wrote in another epistle, "Therefore, if anyone is in Christ, he is a new creation. The old has passed away; behold, the new has come" (2 Corinthians 5:17).

The question is not, "Am I trying hard enough to do good works?" The question is not, "Am I performing all the right rituals in just the right way?" The *real* question is, "Am I a new creation?"

If you are a new creation in Christ, you will stop trying to work your way to God, and you will simply allow God to cleanse you, liberate you, lead you, and form Christ in you. It comes down to a single issue—the issue of the cross. How do you view the cross? How do you view the Lord's death for you on the cross? Was it decisive and complete? Do you believe the Lord's final words on the cross when he said, "It is finished"?

Or is the cross of Jesus Christ somehow not fully adequate for your salvation? Is there something else you need to do in order to complete what the cross of Christ lacks? What can you do to save yourself that Christ has not already done on the cross? John R.W. Stott reminds us:

> Every time we look at the cross Christ seems to say to us, "I am here because of you. It is your sin I am bearing, your curse I am suffering, your debt I am paying, your death I am dying." Nothing in history or in the universe cuts us down to size like the cross. All of us have inflated views of ourselves, especially in self-righteousness, until we have visited a place called Calvary. It is there, at the foot of the cross, that we shrink to our true size.[18]

When we truly realize what Christ has done for us on the cross at Calvary, we want to consecrate every ounce of our energy, every second of our time, every dollar of our earnings to the One who gave everything, even life itself, for us. The grace of God, poured out upon us through the shed blood of Jesus Christ, achieves what law alone could never do.

Grace drives us to offer our all to him.

Notes

1. Richard Dawkins, *The God Delusion* (Boston: Houghton Mifflin, 2006), 283.

2. ProCon.org, "Founding Fathers on Religion in Government," Pros and Cons of Controversial Issues, http://undergod.procon.org/view.resource .php?resourceID=000070.

3. Ibid.

4. Rick Newman, "9 Signs of America in Decline," USNews.com, October 26, 2009, http://money.usnews.com/money/blogs/flowchart/2009/10/26/9 -signs-of-america-in-decline.

5. Charles Krauthammer and Bret Baier, "Future of Manned Space Flight," Fox News Special Report, April 17, 2012, www.foxnews.com/on-air/special -report/2012/04/18/future-manned-space-flight.

6. Eryn Sun, "10 Quotes by John Stott Throughout the Years," *Christian Post*, July 28, 2011, http://www.christianpost.com/news/10-beloved-quotes-by -reverend-john-stott-53021/.

7. Harvard University Library, Page Delivery Service, "Papers Read Before the Association for the Advancement of Women, 1886," p. 7, http://pds.lib .harvard.edu/pds/view/2582395?n=21.

8. ACLU, "Passengers' Stories of Recent Travel," ACLU.org, www.aclu.org /passengers-stories-recent-travel/.

9. ACLJ press release, "ACLJ Sues Alabama School District After It Threatens Disciplinary Action Against Student Who Wears Cross Necklace," ACLJ.org,

October 12, 2000, www.aclj.org/News/Read.aspx?ID=239; WorldNetDaily, "Teacher Orders Third-Grader: Put Bible Away!" WND.com, December 16, 2009, www.wnd.com/2009/12/119214/; Jay Sekulow, "ACLU: The Prayer Censors," ACLJ.org, December 3, 2006, http://aclj.org/school-prayer/aclu-the-prayer-censors.

10. Ernie Suggs, "Atlanta OKs Surveillance Center; Cameras to Watch City," *Atlanta Journal-Constitution*, July 18, 2011, www.ajc.com/news/atlanta/atlanta-oks-surveillance-center-1024743.html.

11. www.foxnews.com/us/2012/08/05/arizona-man-sent-to-jail-for-holding-bible-studies-in-his-home/.

12. Randy Alcorn, "Can God Forgive Abortions?" Eternal Perspective Ministries, EPM.org, March 5, 2010, www.epm.org/resources/2010/Mar/5/can-god-forgive-abortions/.

13. Warren W. Wiersbe, *The Wiersbe Bible Commentary: The Complete New Testament* (Colorado Springs: David C. Cook, 2007), 576; emphasis in the original.

14. Ibid.

15. Ibid.

16. John R.W. Stott, *The Message of Galatians*, The Bible Speaks Today (Downers Grove, IL: InterVarsity Press, 1968), 151.

17. Ibid.

18. Ibid., 179.

About Michael Youssef

Michael Youssef was born in Egypt and came to America in his late twenties in 1977. He received a master's degree in theology from Fuller Theological Seminary in California and a PhD in social anthropology from Emory University. Michael served for nearly ten years with the Haggai Institute, traveling around the world teaching courses in evangelism and church leadership to church leaders. He rose to the position of managing director at the age of thirty-one. The family settled in Atlanta, and in 1984, Michael became a United States citizen, fulfilling a dream he had held for many years.

Dr. Youssef founded The Church of The Apostles in 1987 with fewer than forty adults with the mission to "equip the saints and seek the lost." The church has since grown to a congregation of over three thousand. This church on a hill was the launching pad for Leading The Way, an international ministry whose radio and television programs are heard by millions at home and abroad.

For more on Michael Youssef, The Church of The Apostles, and Leading The Way, visit apostles.org and www.leadingtheway.org.

Leading the Way Through the Bible Commentary Series

About the Series: The Leading the Way Through the Bible commentary series will not only increase readers' Bible knowledge, but it will motivate readers to apply God's Word to the problems of our hurting world and to a deeper and more obedient walk with Jesus Christ. The writing is lively, informal, and packed with stories that illustrate the truth of God's Word. The Leading the Way series is a call to action—and a call to the exciting adventure of living for Christ.

LEADING THE WAY THROUGH DANIEL

Daniel lived as an exile in a hostile country, yet when he committed himself in faith to serve his limitless God, he achieved the impossible. How did Daniel maintain his bold witness for God in spite of bullying and intimidation? How did he prepare himself for the tests and temptations of life?

Like Daniel, believers today live in a culture that is hostile to biblical values. It takes great courage and faith to live as followers of Christ in a post-Christian world characterized by moral depravity, injustice, idolatry, and more. In *Leading the Way Through Daniel*, Michael Youssef passionately shows readers that the resources Daniel relied on are equally available to them.

Sound teaching, vibrant illustrations, and a brisk conversational style will enable readers to take the truths of the book of Daniel and apply them to the pressures, trials, and temptations they face in today's culture.

LEADING THE WAY THROUGH EPHESIANS

Throughout the book of Ephesians, Paul refers to "the riches of God's grace," "our riches in Christ," and "the riches of his glory" as he reminds believers of the spiritual treasures they already possess in Christ.

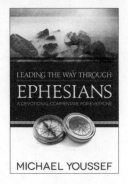

Leading the Way Through Ephesians applies these great truths in such practical areas of the Christian life as

- enduring trials, suffering, and persecution
- maintaining the unity of the church through Christian love
- living out the gospel in our marriages and family relationships
- praying with power
- maintaining our armor against the attacks of Satan

Through sound teaching, vibrant illustrations, a brisk conversational style, and a discussion guide that applies God's truth to the realities of the twenty-first century, *Leading the Way Through Ephesians* will show readers the way to a stronger, more active, more dynamic faith.

LEADING THE WAY THROUGH JOSHUA

The book of Joshua contains some of the most compelling and relevant truths for our lives today. It is the story of "trembling heroes"—people filled with fear who overcame those fears and accomplished the impossible through reliance on God.

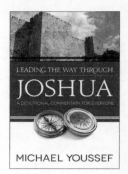

In *Leading the Way Through Joshua,* Michael Youssef translates the challenges Joshua and the nation of Israel faced into challenges that are familiar to everyone. God calls people to follow him, to conquer the Jerichos in their lives, to stand against the idolatry in our land. God calls Christians to tell the world about his covenant love, expressed through the life, death, and resurrection of his Son, Jesus Christ.

Readers of this devotional commentary will discover how to turn the insights of Joshua into action in their own lives. It will motivate them to step up, to be strong and courageous, to obey God, and to go wherever God sends them.

To learn more about Harvest House books and
to read sample chapters, log on to our website:

www.harvesthousepublishers.com

HARVEST HOUSE PUBLISHERS
EUGENE, OREGON